Counseling in Times of Crisis

RESOURCES FOR
CHRISTIAN COUNSELING

Counseling in Times of Crisis

JUDSON J. SWIHART, Ph.D.
GERALD C. RICHARDSON, D.Min.

RESOURCES FOR
CHRISTIAN COUNSELING

General Editor

Gary R. Collins, Ph.D.

WORD PUBLISHING
Dallas · London · Vancouver · Melbourne

Library of Congress Cataloging-in-Publication Data

Swihart, Judson J.
Counseling in times of crisis.

(Resources for Christian counseling ; v.7)
Includes bibliographies and index.
1. Pastoral counseling. I. Richardson, Gerald, 1937- II. Title.
BV4012.2.S88 1987 253.5 87-6230
ISBN 0-8499-3611-X

Printed in the United States of America

4 5 6 7 8 9 LBM 9 8 7 6 5 4 3 2 1

CONTENTS

EDITOR'S PREFACE

IS IT REALLY POSSIBLE TO UNDERSTAND a crisis until you have had one—or have helped somebody through one?

Recently I was in the midst of a busy day at the office when my wife appeared, unexpectedly, and closed the door behind as she entered. My father had had a heart attack, she told me. Already his heart had stopped once and although my dad was still alive, he was not expected to live until evening.

I felt myself overwhelmed by a flood of emotions and confusing decisions. Who was with my mother? How was she responding? Could I get a plane before midnight? What if I waited to go until morning—would Dad slip away during the night? How long would I be gone? What should I do about the counseling class I was due to teach next hour?

I learned later that my mother spent the long hours of that difficult day with a neighbor and a hospital chaplain. Without denying the reality of my father's critical condition, that chaplain had given support, gentle encouragement, and a lot of unhurried time to help my mother face her crisis.

Many of you who read this book have helped in similar ways. Perhaps more than any other group, pastors and Christian counselors are at the forefront of those who intervene to give help in times of special need. Maybe you have learned from books or courses on crisis counseling, but probably you have discovered (or will discover) that practical experience is needed if you really want to help people in times of great stress.

The authors of this book have had many years of practical experience in helping others cope with crises. Judson Swihart is a professional counselor. Gerald Richardson is a pastor. By combining their crisis counseling experience with their technical knowledge and expertise, these authors have produced a volume that is informative, practical, and relevant.

When the people at Word Books approached me about editing a series of books on counseling, I knew that any book on crisis would have to be special. Bookstores are filled with accounts of personal crises and inspiring stories of how people have overcome adversity. Several volumes on crisis counseling have appeared, even within the past few years, and it would be easy to conclude that this book is "more of the same."

The Resources for Christian Counseling series attempts to do something different. Written by counseling experts, each of whom has a strong Christian commitment and practical counseling experience, these volumes are intended to be examples of accurate psychology and careful use of Scripture. Each is intended to have a clear evangelical perspective, careful documentation, a strong practical orientation, and freedom from the sweeping statements and undocumented rhetoric that sometimes characterize books in the counseling field. Our goal is to provide books that are clearly written, practical, up-to-date overviews of the issues faced by contemporary Christian counselors. All of the Resources for Christian Counseling books have similar bindings and together they will comprise a complete encyclopedia of Christian counseling.

Most of the volumes in this series are written by a single author. It seemed appropriate with this book, however, to combine the skills and knowledge of two writers who, together, bring expertise from theology, social work, psychology, and family studies. I first met Judd Swihart many years ago when we both were students at Purdue. When I invited him to write a book in this series, he told about his collaboration with Jerry Richardson and their work on training others to be crisis counselors. I am delighted that these two men have been willing to share their conclusions in the following pages.

I am grateful for the chaplain and neighbor who were available to help our family in a time of crisis. Hopefully many other chaplains and pastors, neighbors and laypeople, professional counselors and beginners will find useful information in the pages of this book. We all know that crises often come unexpectedly and without warning. It is my prayer that the practical suggestions of Doctors Swihart and Richardson will enable you to minister more effectively when you next are called upon to face or help others deal with a crisis.

Gary R. Collins, Ph.D.
Kildeer, Illinois

INTRODUCTION

THE PHONE RINGS. Someone needs your help. A man, a woman, or a child has experienced a trauma which has collapsed his or her ability to cope. Many of these desperate calls come in the evening, on weekends, even in the middle of the night.

We* believe that pastors and counselors who have a background of information on crisis and crisis counseling techniques will be better able to respond to these calls for assistance. We recognize the extreme importance of sound biblical training and the work of the Holy Spirit in all counseling practices. This is the foundation of your ministry. But by acquiring professional skills and adding them to this spiritual foundation, you can be even more effective in the healing process.[1]

You've probably had at least some training in the general area of counseling. However, crisis counseling is a unique approach to special circumstances. Crisis counseling is a unique ministry in and of itself with particular goals and techniques that apply

*As coauthors we'll refer to ourselves as *we* throughout the book, except when we're referring to case histories or personal examples pertaining to only one of us.

only in the crisis situation. This type of counseling is not simply a compressed version of long-term counseling.[2] The pastor or counselor who is confronted with a crisis situation may be more effective if he or she has an understanding of crises in general, some specific crises, and the techniques of crisis counseling.

In this book we present the dynamics of a crisis, a scriptural view of crises, and then an overview of various categories of crises. The various crises are illustrated by case examples to demonstrate the major issues faced by the person in crisis and to present focal points for intervention. The cases presented are based on actual counseling experiences, and all names have been changed to protect the privacy of the persons involved. Techniques of dealing with crisis are also presented to give direction for dealing directly with those in crisis.

The book is written so that you can better understand the issues confronting those going through a crisis. We hope this will enable you to be a facilitator in helping others toward growth. We hope you will be encouraged and strengthened in being a resource and support person at the pivotal point in people's lives. The body of Christ is to be fitted and joined together in such a way that when there is a crisis for one part, the whole body responds (1 Cor. 12:25, 26). Part of the ministry of the church is to support and encourage one another to the point that others look at the church and say, "how they love one another" (1 Thess. 4:9). We hope that this book will contribute to the ministry of those who are called alongside to help during times of trauma.

We also believe the principles presented will be useful to you in the future as you find yourself facing a crisis, for crises are a part of life. They are not something to be avoided, but rather should be seen as points of movement. The idea is not to try to discover ways to avoid crises, but rather to learn how to utilize them to produce growth rather than dysfunction.[3] If one could find a way to go through life with no crises, that person would be successful only in avoiding real life. Crises are woven into the very tapestry of life itself. In fact, the Bible even teaches that we should be thankful for the trials that crises bring because they open the potential for growth of our faith (James 1:2, 3).

PART ONE

THE FOUNDATION

WE WOULD LIKE TO BEGIN this book by presenting some background information that will lend meaning to the other sections. In this first section we would like to discuss the definition and dynamics of a crisis. In order to understand how to approach and help someone through a crisis, one must have some common agreement as to what events are perceived as constituting a real live crisis.

Although this book is not designed to develop a theology of crisis, we would like to consider what we believe the Bible presents as a basic view of crisis. These first two chapters give the foundation on which the following parts are built.

CHAPTER ONE

THE DYNAMICS OF A CRISIS

THE KNOCK ON THE DOOR was slow and deliberate. Who would be coming to the house in the middle of the afternoon? It wasn't time for the kids to come home from school yet. When Jan opened the door she saw Bill, her husband's construction-crew teammate. Quickly she scanned his face for a clue to this unusual visit. She saw trouble and said, "What's wrong? Has something happened to Don?"

Bill stepped through the open door and cautiously searched for words. As Bill detailed the accident, which had taken Dan's life, Jan could only repeat over and over, "No. No. No. It can't be true."

Within hours, her pastor, family, and friends would be there with comfort, support, and encouragement. In spite of their presence, which she greatly valued, the wound in her heart remained. Her life had been so routine, so filled with the repetition of washing dishes, laundering endless piles of dirty clothes, and driving to the grocery store. Last year she had been enthused about taking a part-time job as a dental assistant. It was good to be back at work now that the children were older. Life had finally settled.

But Jan's life, which had been so established, was suddenly jettisoned like a rocket. She was now headed in a new direction, a direction that she had never anticipated. Had she known what this seemingly average day would bring, she would have started it off differently. She would have insisted that Don have a second cup of coffee at breakfast; she would have put something special in his lunch pail; she would have told him she loved him. Those sentiments were there all along but would now remain unexpressed.

Everyone has faced or will face crises, prompted by those jarring events that send a life careening off in new directions. A crisis event may be a phone call from school telling a woman that her child has been caught with drugs or a visit to the doctor confirming a pregnancy. It may be a call from another company offering a man a new job. It may be an announcement that a couple's best friends are moving to the East Coast, or perhaps an accident that disables a spouse. All of these situations qualify as life crisis events.

What are crises? Are they good or bad? Can they even be considered in terms of good or bad? How does faith affect a crisis and how does a crisis affect faith?

WHAT'S IT ALL ABOUT?

What is a crisis? It may be experienced as an exciting distress, a sleepless night, a time of deep searching, a longing to fill an unfillable void, a knot in the pit of your stomach, a time of panic and hope. It is precipitated by some event that upsets spiritual and emotional equilibrium. Basically it is the disequilibrium produced by a perceived threat or adjustment that we find difficult to handle. Here we emphasize "perceived," because if we think a crisis event is going to occur, we have a crisis whether or not the actual crisis event occurs. If a man thinks his boss is upset with him and is going to fire him, the employee may be in crisis even though the boss has no such intentions.[1]

Essentially crisis events are changes in our world that necessitate emotional adjustment on our part. Usually they are produced by sudden and unexpected events; sometimes, however, they are produced by anticipated happenings. Entering into a marriage may be a planned event, yet may cause a crisis. Entering a long-sought retirement can bring about a crisis even though it has been visible in one's future like the finish line banner on a race course. Regardless of whether the event is anticipated or unexpected, the crisis will call for the person to make some adjustment within a matter of a few weeks.

The Precipitating Event

The stress charts indicate that some crisis events generally cause more stress than others. There are mild crisis events and then there are intensive events. The following are among the most stressful crisis events: (1) death of spouse, (2) divorce, (3) marital separation, (4) jail term, (5) death of family member, (6) personal injury or illness, (7) marriage, (8) job loss, (9) marital reconciliation, and (10) retirement.[2]

What happens when we are hit with one crisis event and then, before we have adjusted to it, we have a second or third? The stress compounds! We are at even higher risk for depression or mental disorganization. We are prepared to deal with some level of stress, but there is a point at which the accumulation of stress overwhelms us. We especially need to tune into and be prepared to offer support and encouragement to these people who are experiencing accumulated stressful life events.

Beyond the Event Itself

The onset of certain events creates stressors that may result in the person's coping resources being overwhelmed, resulting in crisis behavior. Lydia Rapoport has observed, "There are three sets of interrelated factors that can produce a state of crisis: (1) a hazardous event which poses some threat, (2) a threat to the instinctual needs which are symbolically linked to earlier threats, and (3) an inability to respond with adequate coping mechanisms."[3] Her statement well summarizes various influences that affect the amount of stress a person feels in a certain situation. These influences include:

1. Past life experiences
2. Social support
3. Coping skills
4. Perception of the crisis
5. World view
6. Understanding the purpose of the crisis
7. Creative solutions

Past life experiences. Certainly, early life experience plays a part in the amount of stress generated by a crisis. If, for example, a man who lost his mother early in life now faces the threat of loss of nurturance, the crisis will cause him a great deal of stress. If, on the other hand, he had positive experiences with self-worth, nurturance, role mastery, and identity earlier in his life, the crisis will be easier.[4] As a counselor you need to help him understand that he has some personal control over his destiny so he need not be overwhelmed by helplessness and hopelessness.

Social support. The stress of a crisis situation can be reduced if a person is part of a group of people that expresses emotional and spiritual support. Those who attempt to go through a crisis alone are more apt to suffer long-term adverse effects than those who have social support.

Coping skills. The skills and ability to cope with stress developed in previous situations may be very useful in new situations. People who have developed good coping skills have an array of possible alternatives for dealing with the current crisis. These skills help the person regain internal stability although the crisis event continues to affect him or her.

Norman Wright, in his very helpful book, *Crisis Counseling*, has identified several personality characteristics of people who are likely candidates for crises because of inadequate coping abilities. Such people:

1. are emotionally weak ("nearly overwhelmed in a crisis")
2. are in poor physical condition
3. deny reality
4. demonstrate oral fixation
5. are unrealistic in timing and time allocation
6. carry excessive guilt
7. blame others for what goes wrong
8. are excessively dependent or independent.[5]

Characteristics identified by Wright are often found in people who seem not to have fully developed into emotional maturity. Erikson stated two reasons for developmental arrest: ineffective parenting and lack of support for development.[6]

Perception of the crisis. In many areas we are not in agreement with Albert Ellis, but we do find some of his concepts very useful. We particularly value his thesis that events do not "cause" feelings; one's feelings are not generated by an event. There is an intermediary step: what one tells oneself about the event. Feelings are based on what one tells oneself, rather than on the event itself.[7]

A. B. C.
Event → What one tells oneself about the event → Feelings

For example, John's doctor asks that John come in for a checkup. For many this would not precipitate a crisis. However, for John it does. Why? Because John tells himself that the doctor's request is a sure sign that John is dying of cancer; he's sure the doctor just wants to confirm it. It is not the event that brings the crisis, but what John tells himself that produces the feelings of anxiety.

The manner in which the crisis is interpreted has much to do with the stress that it generates. The apostle Paul sat in jail (a very big crisis on the stress charts) and sang songs. We don't think that Paul was denying his situation. We don't think Paul was above being human. The difference was in his perception of the situation. Paul was a man whose life was loaded with crises. He had seen and participated in killing a man (Steven), been shipwrecked (that must have been a terrorizing experience), and was beaten and thrown out of town. He apparently grew through his crises, because he saw them as being part of a larger picture in his life and his ministry.

World view. A person's world view also gets involved. What are his or her basic beliefs about life? Does he or she think there is a purpose to the crisis? Can there be growth through the crisis? Does God care about us in a crisis? Is this punishment? If a client maintains a world view that includes some possibility of control by a loving God, the return to equilibrium can be more rapid.

It should be apparent that crises do not necessarily indicate God's favor or punishment. Interpreting a crisis in this manner may only increase the pressure or stress. Throughout the crisis believers have a Comforter in the Holy Spirit and can find comfort from other Christians. God's goodness can come about through any situation. If a client does not have firmly in mind the concept of "God is good," then the perception of the crisis can run off in many directions that usually lead into blind alleys.

Understanding the purpose. Understanding a crisis in terms of its having a purpose can remarkably alter the stress that the events produce. Our visual image of Paul singing in prison illustrates this as well as any example we can think of.

Creative solutions. The last factor affecting the level of stress may be a person's ability to creatively discover appropriate solutions to the crisis event. The emphasis here is on the word "appropriate." David, while in the midst of a crisis with Bathsheba, inappropriately tried to solve his crisis by putting Uriah to death, which in turn only escalated the situation into a bigger crisis. Creativity of solutions is an asset only if the solutions bring a sense of relief.

In our society people tend to resort to various unhelpful methods to deal with a crisis. Some may try to "cope" with the crisis by overactivity. They keep very busy so that they don't have to think about it. For example, people under stress may throw themselves into their work, go out every evening, and get involved in every imaginable activity.

Sometimes people cope by blaming others. (There is a point in the adjustment process where they may need to blame others, but this is only a phase beyond which they need to move.)

Some people may become depressed and physically ill. This should signal a need for support. In some crisis situations it may indicate repression of grief. Others may hold their grief inside until the internal pressure becomes too great. They are at risk of becoming psychotic, suicidal, or even homicidal. Sometimes we see people who become confused to the point that they cannot work or relate to others. This state is more commonly known as a nervous breakdown. Often when the onset of a nervous breakdown has been the result of a sudden crisis, the prognosis is good and the recovery is fairly rapid.

Steps on the Road to Crisis

The movement into a crisis state often occurs in an identifiable sequence.[8]

1. A person's usual life of well-being is distressed by an event that is perceived as a hazard. The level of tension shoots upward.

2. A person makes attempts to cope and regain stability using usual coping skills. He or she realizes this is not working and inner turmoil escalates. He or she will then attempt to eliminate the crisis or escape from it.

3. The usual coping skills are not effective and a person becomes even more fearful, beginning to mobilize inner strengths. During this phase friends are called on for help. This is now a full-blown crisis!

4. If within a couple of months attempts to resolve the crisis fail, the person reaches a breaking point of disorganization. At this point the crisis is so large that the "victim" is overwhelmed and ineffective. He or she may lash out in all directions but accomplish little or become depressed and sit and do nothing at all. Those who end up in this state are described as having a nervous breakdown. Effective crisis counseling is designed to try to prevent this from occurring.

For example, a young wife who went through these steps could not seem to get off her crisis course. She had felt marital tension beyond her ability to cope. The tension built. When she realized she was being ineffective, she moved out of the house. Then she was under even more pressure and began to use all of her resources. Within a few days, as it became obvious that she was still not relieving her stress, she placed her child in another state with her husband's parents. She tried working; she tried moving in with another man; she moved out of the state. Moving back home with her mother she made an effort to sort through her confusion. Not until several months later did she return, pick up her child, and begin to reorganize her life.

One hopes that within a few weeks a new level of stability is established. This level may be regressive or one that has elevated the person's ability to deal with life's stresses. It is critical that you, a pastor or counselor, be able to help others toward growth during this very critical time in their lives.

Loss

Most crises involve a tremendous sense of loss. Lydia Rapoport has suggested that the emotions produced by a crisis depend upon the situation and the perceived loss.[9] She would propose that if an event threatens an instinctual need or affects one's integrity, the person will usually experience anxiety. If the loss or crisis event effects some deprivation, then generally the person will experience depression. Other researchers feel the type of intense emotion experienced in times of crisis may also be related to the personality of the individual. Of course the emotion may be a combination of both anxiety and depression.

Human life is so complex that it's generally impossible to predict a distinctive pattern of response to a crisis event. However, stressful life events long have been recognized as a contributing factor in the development of many physical and psychological disorders. When a counselor notes a crisis event, he or she often will note the development of a physical or psychological symptom which indicates underlying stress. Physical symptoms of sleeplessness, not eating, illness, and headaches are common as are psychological symptoms of anxiety, depression, despair, or confusion. The symptom may not be alleviated until the counselee has resolved the crisis emotionally.

When you learn of someone going through a crisis and you want to help, you need to think of his or her situation in terms of the perceived sense of loss. The loss may be a loss of self-esteem, identity, role mastery, or nurturance.

Self-Esteem

The loss is usually focused on one of several areas. Part of it will involve a loss of self-esteem. The person who loses a job may wonder, *What will others think of me now? Am I a failure? Will my friends still value me as much as they did before?* Most people spend a lifetime attempting to build personal worth. This issue, therefore, becomes especially critical in any crisis.

Bob had held a steady job all his life. He took a position with a company right out of high school and then moved a few times as he got the opportunity to better himself. Eventually he was a foreman. But then he started having disagreements with the assistant manager and consequently was told that due to financial cutbacks they were going to have to let him go. He knew, however, that the real issue was his conflict with the plant manager.

Bob had to work through some difficult feelings as the crisis settled into his life. He described the shock, but was also surprised that he had lost his self-confidence. He was frightened of job interviews, questioned his abilities, and blamed himself for standing up to the manager. In counseling with him one could clearly see the loss of self-worth. Some sleepless nights, some encouragement from his wife, some support from others, some long days of self-examination followed his last paycheck. Fortunately for Bob, he was a capable man and within a month had located a new job. A year later, with a position in which he felt success, his self-confidence had been strengthened once again

Another aspect of loss associated with self-esteem is loss of acceptance. When a life event occurs that could result in a loss of acceptance, people usually become anxious. This is because self-worth seems to be based on both self-acceptance and self-confidence. The crisis can arouse feelings recorded earlier in life around the issues of feeling valued and accepted by parents. The other component of self-confidence is based on feeling some sense of achievement in life. Most crises involve one or both of these issues. It then follows that people with low self-worth or those who struggle the most with this issue of self-acceptance will more frequently be in crisis, as they are most prone to perceive circumstances as being out of control. Their internal balance will be more easily and more extensively upset.

Identity

Crisis events can also bring a loss of identity. For some people, changes bring a reevaluation of who they are. The threat of loss of identity can send shock waves through their systems that their usual defense mechanisms cannot handle. If you have been a grade school teacher all your life, and this profession becomes an important part of how you define yourself to others, what do you do when you retire and lose your identity? Or suppose a woman has been a full-time mother for twenty-four years. People daily have referred to her as "Mom." Her life has been a full-scale attempt to be a good mom and she values herself because she has been a good mom. Now her last child moves a thousand miles away. Who is she? In contemporary society one's identity gets strongly tied to the roles we have occupied. When a person experiences a major role change, the sense of identity is lost. A crisis may force people to deal with this loss and face new discovery, new searching, new growth.

Role Mastery

Another loss concerns role mastery. A man may work and work and refine and refine a certain task. Eventually, he is comfortable. He knows the skill, understands it, and has mastered it. He has a sense of security about this area of his life. Suddenly he is transferred and has to learn a new machine. He no longer has a role in which he believes himself to be competent. A couple who have prided themselves in being good parents suddenly discover their kids are taking drugs. They lose their sense of role mastery. The same might be true of a carpenter who loses the use of his hand or a wife who loses her husband. All have to deal with this sense of loss of a known and comfortable role. They lose a sense of security in that they can no longer be secure in achievement of a specific task or role.

For years Meredith had been an office manager. The days were hectic but she had learned how to run an efficient office and she had the skills to make sure the secretaries accomplished their work. She had not planned to retire for a number of years, but then came the stroke. She recovered fairly well and could walk with the use of a cane, yet she could not keep up with the pressure of the office without the risk of another stroke. Since she had centered her life around being office manager, she went through a very great loss as she could no longer perform in a capacity where she had felt great success. Life would bring new opportunities and two years later she would be delighted in managing the church office, but for the present that remained an unknown future.

Nurturance

Frequently one of the major aspects that generates a crisis is the threat of loss of nurturance. People literally cannot survive their early years without nurturance. As they are taught to be independent to some extent, there still remains that awareness of the need to be loved. There remains a need for nurturance from others. One of the most basic human needs, as basic as the need for food and shelter, is the need to be part of a group.

Whenever there is a threat to this basic need for nurturance, a crisis occurs. The extent of the crisis will depend on how much nurturance has been given by a departing person and on the amount of nurturance needed. Dr. Holmes and Dr. Rahe have developed charts that indicate that the greatest amounts of stress come into people's lives through the experience of loss of a significant other—usually a spouse. If a person becomes one with another person and loses him or her, a cataclysmic response can be expected. The more one is a part of a support network and is surrounded by others who provide support and nurturance, the less the long-term effects of the crisis.

In our own bodies when one organ doesn't function, others increase their output to compensate for the loss. If we lose our sight, our sense of hearing is heightened. In a similar fashion, when one person loses a significant other, the body of believers can compensate for some of the loss by increasing their nurturance and support.

The Effects of Crisis

We like to compare people to triangles. (See figure below.) Under normal conditions their bases rest on stable planes. But when crises come along, these people–triangles are tipped on their points, becoming very unstable. Within a matter of weeks a triangle will fall back onto its base again. But it will not land at the same place on the plane as it previously was. It will move in one of two directions: toward growth and better functioning or toward dysfunction. On occasion, as a result of a crisis a person will grow in some areas and slip backwards in others, but there is usually a general pattern toward either growth or dysfunction.

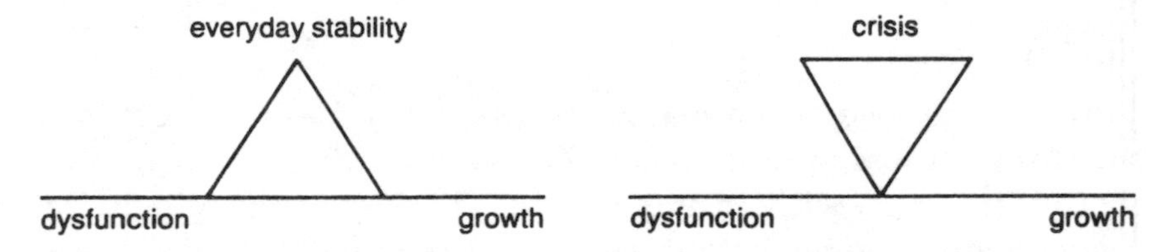

The few weeks following a crisis are extremely important, as the triangle is teetering on its point. Life-long scars can be formed during this time, but, on the other hand, phenomenal healing and growth can be taking place. These are the critical pivotal points in people's lives. Perhaps it is no mistake that the Chinese characters that represent the word *crisis* mean both "danger" and "opportunity."[10] During the first four to six weeks following a crisis you as a counselor can play a prime part in enhancing the growth of a client. You will want to see people in crisis move toward growth rather than dysfunction.[11]

Although there remains much developmental work to be done, our approach to crisis intervention has been constructed by pulling together concepts from a variety of theoretical perspectives and various disciplines to form what is known as "crisis counseling techniques."

Reach Out

When you become aware of someone going through a potentially stressful life event or dealing with physical or psychological symptoms, reach out to him or her. Remember, the person is at a turning point and you have the opportunity to assist in facilitating growth. You cannot do everything and you cannot cause his or her triangle to move toward dysfunction or growth. People and their crises are too complex for that. As a counselor you are not single-handedly responsible for their growth or lack of growth; so don't think of yourself in an unrealistically lofty position.

A good model for your interaction is the one provided by the ministry of the Holy Spirit. Perhaps you can be one who comes alongside to offer help. In love you give the most support you possibly can. Realize that, although most of the time people in crisis will absorb your support and comfort, there *will* be times when some people will not. They will struggle through the crisis or it may even get worse before it gets better. You can only offer your support. You cannot force the triangle in one direction or the other. What you *can* do, however, is offer those in crisis a very important resource that they desperately need—an attitude. The attitude that one chooses to use in facing a crisis can make all the difference in the world. It is attitude that can turn a crisis into either a tragedy or a growth-producing experience.[12] By your approach you model for them an attitude—what a great gift for those in need.

CHAPTER TWO

A BIBLICAL VIEW OF CRISIS

FROM COVER TO COVER the Bible is filled with illustrations of people in crisis. At times in great detail, it describes how they perceived and dealt with trauma. In its pages we get numerous pictures of an individual's or a group's perception of a crisis. We see the spiritual impact of crisis and often the effectiveness of various behaviors for dealing with it. From the violence in Cain and Abel's family to the disciples' fear when they believed their boat was ready to sink, crises permeate the Scriptures. In this chapter we would like to present a foundation of scriptural insights and then consider resources available to Christians responding to crisis events and responding to others in crisis.

UNDER GOD'S DOMINION

We hold the perspective that God created the world, is over the world, and holds the world together. Therefore, crisis needs to be perceived as being under the dominion of God. It is not within the scope of this book to develop a theology of crisis, nor a theology of the role of God's sovereignty, but we would like to look briefly at the origins of crisis events. Such an overview will help you consider crisis in terms broader than the question, *Which technique should I use with which crisis?* Biblical principles are needed, but within the setting of a biblical view of crisis.

As the following diagram shows, we see crisis events as having one of three origins: (1.) They are produced by the specific direction of God. (2.) They come about as a result of the natural progression of creation. (3.) They may be a result of spiritual deprivation, our own or that of others.

Origin of Crisis

Specific Direction of God	Natural Progression of Creation	Spiritual Deprivation
For example:	For example:	For example:
job loss/gain	natural disaster	crime victim
moving	death	disappointment in spiritual leader
marriage	birth of child	rape
conversion	aging and sickness	financial loss
	hospitalization	
	launching children	

Specific Direction

Some crises may originate as a result of the specific intervention of God in a person's life.

There once was an angry man whose purpose was clear: to get rid of the troublemakers. Something had to be done to protect his religion, his very way of life. The man was no crazy man; he was, after all, one of the best-educated men of his time. This man was a leader in every sense of the word. Suddenly, as this man was marching toward his target, a light from the sky engulfed him. Talk about a crisis event! In fear, this stubborn, iron man fell to the ground. He heard a voice, "Saul, Saul, why are you persecuting me?"

Saul almost automatically cried back in fear, "Who art thou, Lord?"

The voice from heaven responded, "I am Jesus whom you are persecuting." Saul was then told to rise and go to the city for which he had originally set out and await instructions. The Bible tells us in the ninth chapter of Acts that even Saul's traveling companions "stood speechless, hearing the voice, but seeing no one."

What a sudden change! From confidence and self-righteous rage these men became humble, confused, and aware of their vulnerability.

Most Christians refer to the encounter of Saul, later called Paul, on the road to Damascus as his "conversion experience." He certainly was a changed person from that point forward. But the Damascus encounter was also a crisis of major proportions. God still intervenes in people's lives, calling them forward with specific direction.

Christians need a constant openness to God's call even though it may involve change.

We are taught to follow the leading of the Holy Spirit. Will doing this lock us into one task for the rest of our lives or even a number of years? It might mean that, but it most likely will mean monumental change. We are taught that the Holy Spirit is like a wind that blows wherever it wills. The New Testament is depicting a lifestyle of change, change, and more change. Too often we are led in a new direction, move there, get our lives stabilized, and then balk at moving when led in another direction. We have our homes, our friends, our paychecks, our favorite stores. The thought of uprooting any or part of our lives seems difficult. Another possibility is that we get a fine program moving or a successful business. Before long the ego gets involved, as we all like to be viewed as "successful." Then we are called to some new situation but hesitate to give up that which is going along so well.

But think back on some responses to God's specific direction: A few apparently successful fishermen were willing to go through crisis in order to respond to Jesus' call to be fishers of men. An apparently successful carpenter was willing to flee from Bethlehem to Egypt with his wife and infant son. A well-educated Roman citizen was willing to become a traveling missionary. All these experienced some degree of crisis, but they held in common a willingness to follow the direction of the calling of God in their lives.

Natural Progression of Creation

God is a God of change. Change is a part of the universe he created. Why do rugged mountains wear down to smooth hills? Why are there seasonal changes in climate? Why does the wind change direction? Why did God create caterpillars that grow into beautiful butterflies? Why did he create each day different from the last? Each day the sunset changes so there have never been two just alike. Although he remains constant, does this not speak clearly of a God who values change in his created world?

Many of the life-cycle crises come about as a result of this natural progression in creation. Some health crises are related to the whole concept of aging and cell reproduction and replacement. Floods, earthquakes, and fires can be occasions of crisis. Empty nests and retirements can also be prompted by natural progression. This is the way God in his infinite wisdom decided to create our physical bodies and environments.

Spiritual Deprivation

All of us experience some crises that result from a fallen world system and/or our own sin. Through personal sin King David brought extreme crisis into his own life as well as the lives of others. Other biblical characters, such as Stephen, faced the crisis of death because they resided in a fallen world.

No doubt you will be called upon frequently to provide assistance to those who experience crisis originating out of the results of sin. Those who are victims of crime, those in emotional trauma, those going through divorce, those who have been raped, those who have experienced some major financial loss may be experiencing crisis originating from within this category.

All Have a Purpose

From a biblical basis, we do not want to consider a crisis as being good or bad in terms of its origin. Crises are a part of the very fabric of life and cannot be avoided. We can better accept the crisis event when we understand that there is a reason for the event that goes beyond the event itself. God is a God of purpose and is very specific in relationship to his universe. He uses crisis events as tools for carrying forth his purpose even when the purpose is not clear to us.

A crisis event is often a change in our world that forces us to change in order to accommodate a new set of circumstances. We may accept the event as ultimately within the plan of God or we may harden ourselves and resist the inevitable. Adjustment comes as we begin to accept the idea that things are different and will never be the same. What the crisis event does is to put us into a position of choice, and either we resist or accept. It is the person's response to the crisis event that becomes a critical matter both spiritually and emotionally. In the end we have to make our choice: to respond to crisis events with spiritual maturity and resources or to deal with them on our own, in our own might.

Spiritual Resources

Providentially, God did not leave the world without spiritual resources that help us face crisis events. We would like to consider five spiritual resources. When counseling you will want to draw your clients' attention to any or all of these resources.

The Character of God

Those who have chosen to believe in the Bible and place their faith in Christ have access to the character of God. Whatever the crisis, the bottom line is that *God is good.* This aspect of God's character helps to correct the inner imbalance produced by the crisis events (Rom. 8:31, 32). During these times of despair and desperation, people need to be able to cling to the truth of this aspect of God's character.

Solomon, as recorded in 1 Kings 8:22–24, proclaimed the trustworthiness of God as he reminded the children of Israel of God's faithfulness to them as a people. The children of Israel could have shared our motto: "In God we trust" (although they, like we, might more accurately have said, "In God we trust—most of the time").

If crisis and sudden change creates insecurity (which it does in most if not all cases), then reinforce the truth that ultimate security, that which is unchangeable, is God himself. To grow in relationship with him, people must change to be more like him, as he is the same yesterday, today, and forever (Heb. 13:8). When a person knows God is love and that he will never change, he or she has a sense of security unmatched by any aspect of a world that is in a state of constant change.

Young Timmy was what you'd call a normal boy, but he had a terminal illness. It seemed to be one of those "it isn't fair" cases. He had accepted Jesus Christ as his Lord in Sunday school, and shortly before he died his mother asked me to baptize Timmy in the hospital. I went immediately and before I baptized him I asked Timmy if he knew the Lord. He mustered his strength and surprised me by almost shouting yes. After baptizing him in the name of the Father, the Son, and the Holy Spirit, I wondered, *Why Timmy?* But I knew that he knew what to expect and where he wanted to be—at his eternal home.

When preparing Timmy's funeral service I wept, grieving the loss of a young friend, but also feeling the sadness of his family and those who had treated him. Because of this young man many heard of Jesus Christ. Timmy's earthly life was short but meaningful. He faced his crisis because of his relationship with Jesus Christ. I believe he has a crown of righteousness that will be given him at the judgment seat of Christ.

Direction

The Bible is not necessarily a book of rules, but it does give us direction. Humans are not left groping in a fog to come up with their own definitions of right and wrong.[1] We do have principles and guidelines that apply. Although the guidelines are at times difficult to apply to gray areas, they do exist.

The Bible provides not only direction for behavior, but direction for thought patterns concerning crisis (Prov. 16:3).

Applicable references are numerous, but the following are just a few you might suggest your clients read or memorize.

> Yet in all these things we are more than conquerors through Him who loved us. For I am persuaded that neither death nor life, nor angels nor principalities nor powers, nor things present nor things to come, nor height nor depth, nor any other created thing, shall be able to separate us from the love of God which is Christ Jesus our Lord. (Rom. 8:37–39)

> Peace I leave with you, My peace I give to you; not as the world gives do I give to you. Let not your heart be troubled, neither let it be afraid. (John 14:27)

> But now in Christ Jesus you who once were far off have been made near by the blood of Christ. For He Himself is our peace, who has made both one, and has broken down the middle wall of division between us. (Eph. 2:13, 14)

> Be anxious for nothing, but in everything by prayer and supplication, with thanksgiving, let your requests be made known to God; and the peace of God which surpasses all understanding, will guard your hearts and minds through Christ Jesus. (Phil. 4:6, 7)

We encourage the use of specific Scriptures for specific emotions such as fear, depression, and weakness. The appendix of this book includes a helpful and longer list of Scriptures categorized to specific emotions.

The Power of Prayer

God does move through the power of prayer—if the prayers are within the confines of his will. It is so easy for a person to pray, "God, get me out of this mess," rather than to pray, "Help me know you and be sensitive to your leading through this crisis."

Prayer brings God into the crisis. Think again of what happened to Israel when they were between the Egyptian army and the Red Sea. In this case, God miraculously removed the danger. But God never acts the same way twice. He allowed Daniel to sit in the lions' den and Paul in prison—yet both men had a peace that held firm through the crisis event.

The Comfort of the Holy Spirit

One of the tasks of the Holy Spirit is to be our Comforter. This is a remarkable spiritual resource. It allows people to experience anxiety and yet maintain an inner peace that passes human understanding.

Some theorists have recognized the value of faith for emotional adjustment but have come short of fully appreciating the work of the Holy Spirit. They say, "Religion gives an individual a chance to face life's problems with greater confidence and develops an attitude that will serve in time of crisis."[2] This commonly held view is generally true, but it deals with religion as opposed to a relationship with Jesus Christ which we have because the Spirit of Christ dwells within us.

One Gospel writer records Jesus' very last words as, "I am with you always, even to the end of the age" (Matt. 28:20). Jesus said this knowing he was sending the Holy Spirit to dwell in people's hearts. The writer of Hebrews quotes Jesus as saying, "I will never leave you nor forsake you." Because Jesus said that, we can say, "The Lord is my helper; I will not fear. What can man do to me?" (Heb. 13:5, 6). The key to Christianity's approach to crisis is not religion per se; rather, it is a relationship with Jesus Christ—through the Holy Spirit.

The secular world all too often views Christianity's value mainly in the context of rituals such as marriage or funerals.[3] While the rituals used by the church do serve a useful purpose, the primary value of the church is not its rituals but the relationship with Christ and the work of the Holy Spirit to which it speaks—even in its rituals.[4]

This spiritual resource—the presence and comfort of the Holy Spirit—is not always given adequate consideration since it is spiritual rather than visible, but one must not underestimate its value (Rom. 8:26).

The Body of Christ

God created believers to live in fellowship, to support and edify one another. This is very apparent when it comes to crises, especially one in which pain is involved. God gave different members of the body different gifts so that each would need to live in a state of interdependency (1 Cor. 12:12). If one part of the body hurts, the entire body should reflect the pain (1 Cor. 12:26). One part of the body cannot fully function apart by itself, but only in relationship to the rest of the body.

Christ talked a great deal about what it meant to be a Christian. He puzzled many people by telling them that it was not just following a set of laws (Matt. 7:12) but that it had to do with the love they demonstrated in their lives (Luke 10:27, 28).

They were told to focus their attention on people, not on things (Matt. 6:19–21). They were told they should love their neighbor as themselves. When asked who was their neighbor, Jesus told them of the Samaritan who went out of his way to meet the needs of someone in crisis (Luke 10:25–37). The Samaritan did not judge the suffering man for having needs, nor did he try to assess whether or not the man deserved his help. He simply offered assistance. When asked about the most important aspects of the Christian life, Jesus said the greatest was that you "love the LORD your God with all your heart, with all your soul, with all your mind, and with all your strength." The second commandment was, "You shall love your neighbor as yourself" (Mark 12:30, 31).

How can you demonstrate your love for others? There are many ways God leads people to express this love. Basically, Christians want their lives to count for something. They want a purpose to their lives; they desire that their lives be more than a noisy gong or clanging cymbal (1 Cor. 13:1). They look around them and find ways of expression. But in some areas there is still room for improvement. Christians can become even more effective in fulfilling their desire to be an example of God's love in the world. One of the greatest demonstrations of love is reaching out to those who are going through a crisis—their moment of tremendous need.

We desire that the world look at our lives and not see man burdened down by many laws (Luke 11:39–47), but rather that they marvel at the way we love one another (1 Thess. 4:9). Once we can understand how the emotional and spiritual upheaval in our lives has produced growth in our relationship with God we may eventually even be thankful for the event occurring. We may not be thankful for the pain of the event, but for the growth which is now in our lives that would not be there without it.

SUMMARY

From an overview of Scripture our perspective of crisis is as follows:

1. Crisis events are a part of life originating from God's specific direction, the natural progression of creation, or humanity's spiritual deprivation.
2. There is a purpose for the crisis event (Prov. 16:9). God is a God of purpose and direction, even when we in finite wisdom do not understand his mind (Prov. 30:3, 4).
3. The crisis can be an opportunity for resistance to change (Pharaoh and the plagues [Exod. 5–12]) or change can ultimately be accepted (Rom. 8:31).
4. There are spiritual resources available for dealing with crisis.
5. Ultimately when we understand the crisis we may even be able to thank God for the growth which the crisis event has produced (Rom. 8:28, 37).

As Christians, we have a basis for understanding crisis within the context of faith. As Christian counselors, we need to be able to bring a perspective to those who are in the midst of struggle. We need to develop the ability to interact in ways consistent with Scripture. We need to know how to apply biblical passages as well as quote them. We need to be able to respond with love, compassion, and understanding.

Our desire is that the remainder of this book will help to develop understanding that can be added to biblical perspective in order to assist you in becoming an effective crisis counselor.

PART TWO

THE FRAMEWORK

WE BELIEVE THAT crisis counselors need to approach counseling from a systematic framework. We also think they need to approach those in crisis with a clear understanding of the problems they face. The pastor or other counselor who is providing crisis intervention needs to know what issues and emotions are common to a particular crisis so that he or she approaches each situation knowing what direction to take. We recognize that each situation and each person is unique, but a general pattern will no doubt be present in a healing ministry.

To provide this framework, we have developed categories of crises which will help provide understanding of the crisis situations. Each chapter includes case examples to enhance your empathy and understanding and major issues and emotions on which to focus counseling. These then give direction to the intervention. This section can serve as a reference so that you may approach with confidence crisis situations that you may not have personally experienced.

CHAPTER THREE

HEALTH-RELATED CRISES

THERE IS A CLOSE RELATIONSHIP between our physical, emotional, and spiritual health. In this chapter on health-related crises we shall explore the dynamics of physical and psychological crisis situations.

Most of you have no doubt ministered to patients and their loved ones in a hospital setting. Physical conditions become a crisis experience when the onset of the physical problem is sudden or has a major impact on lives. Additionally, we will explore problems related to disabilities and the crises they often trigger. Finally, we will look at two family crisis situations that are related to physical health: premarital pregnancy and physical abuse or assault.

Hospitalization

Case Example

John has not been feeling well. Like thousands of others, this morning he is being admitted to a hospital. He knows he's going to have a series of tests during the next twenty-four hours. Questions are distressing him: *What will they find? Will I have to have surgery? Do I have cancer?* His mind races over the vast array of imaginable situations. John is in a state of crisis that will continue for some time. The crisis will be increased by hospital procedures and the interaction John has with the staff.

Today John will feel that the hospital has taken control over his body. As John enters the hospital he begins to feel that he is no longer a person. "Please fill out this form," says the attendant at the admissions window. "Be sure to put down your social security number." The old number game will be prevalent: social security card, form number, room number, hospital I.D. bracelet. From person to number, the crisis grows. *Hey somebody out there, I'm John. I am not 900-23-7815, nor am I the gallstone case in room 24.*

After John has proven that he can pay the bill, he is put into a wheelchair and propelled to his room. No sooner does he get acquainted with his new surroundings than the process of testing begins. A needle here, a pulse rate check there, and a blood pressure reading. A series of tests begins to find out why John's body is not working properly. As the number of tests increases and no indication of results is given, John becomes more nervous and upset. He searches the faces and listens to the tone of every word to seek a clue as to the seriousness of his situation.

By nightfall the tests have ended, dinner is served, and a new shift of nurses and aides has come in. John feels that he's had no time to catch his breath. He does know, however, that he is apprehensive. What will the doctor tell him tomorrow morning? With a new bed, strange surroundings, and people coming in to check on him, John does not sleep well.

After what seems like an eternity, the doctor enters his room. There is an obstruction. An operation is needed. As the doctor sits next to him and draws a picture of where the problem is located, John becomes scared. Yet he keeps up a good front. In a few fleeting minutes the doctor is gone, and John tries to deal with his fear alone. Surgery frightens him because that blockage could be cancer and there is some risk that he could even die in surgery. He doesn't know what to do—pray, cry, or curse.

John's family visits him and learns the results. Surgery scares them too. Everyone puts up a brave front for the others. A series of "what ifs" begins to race through each mind. John's crisis has become a crisis for every member of the family.

Early the next morning John's wife visits him. A nurse, whom John now knows by name, gives him a shot. Just after sunrise an orderly arrives with a gurney. There are a few more words, a kiss, a briefly uttered prayer as tears are fought back. John's wife joins the march to the operating theater where the doctors and nurses will perform at what everyone hopes will be their best. As the doors close and John is alone with those whom he gave permission to cut him open, his fear reaches a peak. The anesthetics take over. . . .

While the doctors and staff do their job, John's wife waits in the lobby with a few friends. She, too, is facing one of the most serious crises of her life. Questions go racing through her mind. *What will I do if John dies? If it's cancer, will they get it all? Will he have to live differently?* Thinking she must be strong, she doesn't share these questions with anyone else.

Minutes drag into an hour, two hours, and more. Finally, a gown-clad figure appears. John's wife looks for any facial sign but there is none to read. She is told that John got through the surgery okay but that the obstruction may be malignant. It will be a few days before it can be determined. The doctor feels they have removed the growth; she can go and see John in about an hour. She sighs in relief. She can worry about the future results later, she thinks, because she at least knows that her John is going to be all right for now.

Discussion

The issue of sudden illness is one we cannot overlook in the Gospels, as numerous passages are devoted to healing.[1] Nor can we ignore the importance of the healing ministry of the disciples. In Scripture we have recorded God's constant concern about those who are suffering from physical illness. Pain and discomfort aside, just the fear of going for medical assistance or of a dreaded diagnosis may precipitate a crisis.[2] Not knowing what to expect in the hospital experience, John feared the unknown. As hospital staff and doctors begin to explain the medical situation, a patient's fear will be reduced. Family and close friends of the patient can help by showing their support and concern. The Christian who is hospitalized can be reassured by being aware of the prayers offered on his or her behalf.

A loss of identity is felt by many patients as they are numbered and treated methodically. When hospital staff members use a patient's name and show an interest in the person, much of the loss of identity is reduced.[3] Family and friends help reduce this sense of loss by their phone, mail, or personal contacts.

Surgery often results in the loss of some bodily part. Even a diseased part of the body is a part of the whole. There will be a period of grieving over the loss. This appears to be necessary and normal. The patient needs to be reassured that he or she is still perceived to be a whole person. One of the major threats is that the person may feel as if he or she is not a complete person.[4] The greater and warmer the support given by significant others to the patient, the easier will be this passage through the grief.

Stroke patients and accident victims are among those who most often face the frustration of not being able to do what they've done in the past.[5] This sense of partial or total loss of control over one's body is frightening and frustrating, even when the loss of control is temporary. Pitying or being overly solicitous or helpful can do more damage than good. The patient needs to feel loved, valued, and capable. It is extremely important to allow patients to do as much as possible for themselves.

When John entered the hospital he may have felt a loss of control over his financial affairs. As he completed forms, he was asked, "Who is your insurance carrier?" and "How much will the plan pay?" Some hospitals require deposits which can result in the loss of control of one's savings. After the hospitalization, the patient is faced with paying the bills that were not covered by insurance. Family members can help by gathering information on optional payment programs, methods of getting loans when needed, and reassuring the patient that with time the financial situation will be resolved. There are many organizations that can help in this area of concern, especially with long-term illnesses.

In many cases a breakdown in communications accompanies the crisis. A teenager may find the hospitalized parent intensifying a conflict from the past. Hospital staff members may find patients angry over apparently minor events. Why? Because a patient withdraws and has a negative self-image due to physical loss as well as financial cost. Medications, psychological pressures, and body chemistry imbalances can also intensify interpersonal conflicts. Allowing for those problems, being patient, showing a caring attitude, and using good communication skills can help. As those who around patients are able not to be defensive, some of the pressure build-up can be reduced.

Good communication skills are essential for those who minister to the ill. Body language, especially touch, is important when communicating with people who are sick. Many patients feel comforted and confirmed when their hand is held. Many pastors make it a practice to hold a patient's hand while praying with the person. Of course you can also communicate your care for and appreciation of the patient by words. Many messages need to be repeated for people to believe them. Additionally, effective communications often need clarification. Sometimes a patient hears something other than what is intended. Confirming what is being heard is an essential communication skill.

During John's hospitalization he was faced with his own mortality. The fear of death exists even in well-grounded Christians. Frequently, a patient's stress reactions are stimulated by this fear. Allowing a patient to talk about death can be a helpful way to allow him or her to work through this issue. A patient may express concerns about death, even when facing a minor operation that is not particularly life-threatening. To attempt to discount or pass off this fear is often more damage than help in most cases. As a pastor or Christian counselor, you can be of special help in this area.

John felt abandoned at various times in his hospital confinement. This common feeling is especially significant for the long-term patient. As treatment extends beyond ten days to two weeks, visits, calls, and cards begin to diminish in number. A regular phone call or visit and a periodic note become important for the long-term patient, who may otherwise feel that the church has abandoned him or her.

Often associated with the sense of abandonment is an underlying anger with the unfairness of the hospital confinement. *What did I ever do to deserve this? Why me?* The anger is aimed at hospital staff, doctors, family members, friends, or even God. By human standards, not all of life is fair. Of course, God has an eternal perspective while we have a very limited perspective. As we humans begin to better understand God's perspective, we can better manage the anger of apparent unfairness.

Hospital confinement of children is one of the most serious crisis events families face. Many hospitals have excellent pediatric units with highly qualified professionals staffing the units. Nurses in these units tend to be skilled communicators with children; they show warmth and positive support.

Sometimes parents of hospital-confined children panic. This heightens the child's fear and makes life harder for the medical staff treating the child. It is very important that parents show an extra measure of affection along with a very positive attitude toward the ill child. Children rapidly sense their parents' feelings.

Friends and relatives can add a sense of encouragement through visits, telephone calls, and cards. Most hospitals do not allow young children into hospital rooms to visit (for a number of good reasons), but playmates can call or send cards.

Parents of sick or injured children need a great deal of support. There are few situations that make an adult feel more helpless than the hospital confinement of his or her child. Parents also need to be reassured that they have been fulfilling their parental roles and that their children are all right. Parents, too, need affection, a positive attitude from those around them. Prayer can be of great help to the frightened parent. Helping with child care, meal preparation, and household cleaning is a significant way to demonstrate love and support to a parent.

Common Feelings and Issues for Counselors to Address

- fear of the unknown
- loss of one's identity
- loss of control over one's body
- worry over financial problems resulting from hospitalization
- fear of death
- abandonment
- anger over the perceived unfairness of it all

DISABILITY

Case Example

Most people don't dwell on the fact that they will be disabled several times in their life spans. Such a thought is avoided until we or someone close to us is confronted with a disabling accident or sickness.

For twenty years Ed has left home by sunrise in order to get to his job at the foundry on time. His wife Alice always has gotten up with him to see that he has had a good breakfast and to prepare his sack lunch. This morning is like every work-day morning. Alice kisses Ed as he goes out the front door. They have a good life together. Susan and Ed, Jr., are both in high school and doing well. The family home is modest but comfortable, and the furnishings are attractive. Ed and Alice have set aside over ten thousand dollars in a savings account—to cover any emergency. While the family has two cars in good repair, they are both fairly old. Simply stated, Ed and Alice are doing okay.

Alice is cleaning up the house before lunch when the phone rings. It is Ed's boss. He says that Ed has been involved in an accident and is on his way to the hospital. Alice slowly sets down the phone in a state of shock. "What do I do?" she whispers.

Within minutes, Alice is in her car and headed toward the hospital. Her anxiety is rising with each passing moment.

As she bursts into the emergency room, she recognizes one of Ed's coworkers. Anxiously she asks how Ed is and what happened. Charlie, Ed's fellow worker for several years, tells her that some steel broke loose from its storage place, resulting in several men being pinned. He goes on to report that Ed appeared to have broken both legs and was complaining about pain on his right side. Alice's fears escalate as she hears the report.

She races to the admitting window and demands to see her husband. "Not now," says the attendant in the white uniform. "He's in surgery. I'll call you as soon as the doctor is able to talk to you."

Alice, normally a calm woman, is filled with mountains of confusing emotions. She doesn't know what to do—to cry, scream, or run. Charlie senses her crisis, comes alongside, and puts his arm around her. After a moment they sit down together waiting for word, and Alice lets herself cry.

Two hours later the doctor emerges from the emergency room. He calls Alice's name. Alice and Charlie get up as the tall, balding man walks toward them. "Ed's coming along fine. He's in recovery and you'll be able to see him in an hour or so," says the doctor. Alice asks how he is. The doctor reports that both legs are broken, that he has some internal bruises and a strained back. He goes on to estimate that Ed will be off work for about three months. A near-full recovery could be possible; the injuries to his legs are serious enough to cause a permanent limp, possibly requiring a brace.

Alice feels some relief as she goes back to the couch to sit down and wait to see her husband. A number of disquieting questions go through her mind. *What will happen if Ed can't do the same work anymore? Will we have enough money to cover all our needs? How will I take care of Ed?*

Discussion

That terrifying phone call or a visit by the police reporting an accident or sudden sickness turns the calmest person into a human in crisis. The first element in the forming of the crisis is the very suddenness of the precipitating event. When one is unprepared for an event it takes time to regain composure. It takes time to regroup. Responses may range from an attempt to separate oneself from the event by going into a nearly paralyzed state or by becoming hyperactive.

Once a person has an idea of what he or she is facing, a degree of calmness settles in; yet there are still many questions. *What does the future hold? How can adjustment to the change take place?* Often, estimates of the future are far off the mark.[6]

After they have been released from the hospital most disabled persons continue to need some physical help, which may range from delivering medicines and doing minor chores to being cared for around the clock. The greater the amount of care needed, the greater the stress within the family. Even when medical insurance pays for in-home nursing, some additional help from family members will be necessary. This means family members will have to change their lifestyles in some way.

Some of the adjustment issues faced as a result of the disability are:

1. Who is going to nurse the disabled person when he or she returns home?
2. How are the medical bills going to be paid?
3. Is someone else in the family going to have to begin to work or take a second job?
4. How is the disabled person going to deal with losses during the period of disability?
5. How will the family social system be changed, especially the marriage?
6. Will family members have different feelings about the disabled person?
7. What job changes will face the disabled person?
8. How will the disabled person adjust to changes in his or her physical condition?

With hospital costs per day climbing, even medically insured people have a real incentive to get out of the hospital as fast as possible. Yet hospital costs are not the total picture. Visits to the doctor's office, medicines, physical therapy, in-home nursing, medical equipment and supplies, convalescent care hospitals, and other medical services have escalated to a point that even short-term disabilities can create a financial crisis for the family. If family members have to help out financially, the resentment or disappointment may build. In many cases of long-term disability, families have to take out loans which extend the frustration beyond the term of the disability itself. The other aspect of financial crisis occurs when the disabled person is the principal income source for the family. While worker's compensation, personal injury insurance, or disability coverage may lessen the extent of financial loss, most disabilities will involve some unrecoverable income loss.

The various stresses of long-term disabilities add pressure which result in multiple crises over the life span or the term of the disability. Even the person who "recovers" from a disability may be affected by it for the rest of his or her life. Ultimately, the disabled person needs to work toward two goals: reducing the negative physical effects of the disability (i.e., using physical therapy to allow more freedom) and/or viewing the disability in positive terms.

Many inspiring books have been written about "comebacks" people have made after being disabled. Other stories have been told of people who have found ways to turn their disabilities into advantages. Other people, by changing their view of the disability, have been able to help themselves and others. Even a permanent disability can turn into a victory if viewed from a positive perspective. It may take time and hindsight to realize the apostle Paul was right when he said that "all things work together for good to those who love God" (Rom. 8:28).

The crisis associated with illness or disability affects not only the individual who is the patient; it also has a profound impact on those associated with the patient. They may feel victimized by the "misfortune" of their family member. Anger builds over what the disability is doing to the family members. How can they be angry at someone who is suffering? This anger can generate guilt, which can also develop in the disabled person. Sometimes family members will blame themselves in some way for the disability. Or they may blame the disabled person, feeling his or her carelessness has disrupted the family's lifestyle. The guilt can cause an assortment of changed behavior by the family member, who may attempt to avoid contact with or show anger toward the disabled person. Depression may be apparent. In some cases, the family member may develop an illness or have an accident. Resentment and bitterness are frequently seen.

Children sometimes feel that they are different from other children because they have to help their disabled parents. The impact of the disability may result in children being depressed, angry, or not "normal." Adult children may feel torn between living their own lives and taking care of their disabled parents. They may feel guilty for doing neither as well as they feel they should.

Long-term illnesses and disabilities become a family affair. It can be very important for the disabled person and the family to receive professional counseling. Frequently, the families, pastor, and church members can be of great help. There may even be a time of faith development, as the person experiences the provision of numerous needs. In times of adversity the awareness of provision is acute.

People who have never received enough attention to meet their needs may relish the attention they receive when disabled. They then have more incentive to remain impaired than to recover their full potential. Should this take place, professional help can be sought.

As those who are permanently disabled progress through the stages of loss, they need a sense of hope for the future. They may not be able to emotionally receive hope in the initial stages, but later a word of encouragement needs to be sounded. Even the most seriously disabled person can do a great deal. In a southern California community a once-sighted building contractor continued his business while blind and successfully started an additional business as well. Individuals who have lost limbs have been successful in compensating for those losses and having outstanding careers. The most important goal in dealing with the needs of a disabled person is to achieve the highest and best level of recovery.

Every person is worthwhile. It is essential that we work toward the dignity of each person.

Common Feelings and Issues for Counselors to Address

- uselessness
- loss of control over one's life; vulnerability
- financial dependence; fear of being a financial liability to family
- change of lifestyle for self and significant others
- loss of goals
- shame from a scar or handicap
- nonacceptance by others
- anger and frustration of being a victim
- identity change and crisis
- hopelessness
- other family members' guilt or anger
- other family member feeling like a victim

PREMARITAL PREGNANCY

Case Example

While in high school, Sheri is extremely quiet and not very popular. Because of her religious background and beliefs, she does not enter into many extracurricular activities. Her grades are average, and she has no interest in going to college.

Kathi, Sheri's attractive older sister, is popular in school. Sheri lives in her shadow. Kathi marries the star of the football team a year after graduation. Her husband, a carpenter, works with his father. A year after their marriage Kathi and Art have a baby girl.

Most of what Sheri knows about sex she learned from her sister, Kathi. Her parents never discussed anything about human reproduction with her. In reality, her parents never discussed any issue in depth with their children. They told Sheri what to do, but seldom sought her opinion on any topic. This family seemed to have bought into the idea that children should be seen and not heard. Sheri was never physically or verbally abused, just ignored.

For a while during high school Sheri considers running away from home. But she has nowhere to go. There is no one she feels who really cares for her. Instead of leaving home, she manages to stick it out and dreams of the day when she can start a life of her own.

The summer after graduation Sheri is able to get a job at a local coffee shop. She works for about twenty hours a week and is able to earn almost five hundred dollars a month with tips. Her plans are to buy a car in order to gain a sense of independence. However, when she brings the money home, her parents tell her that they have decided she should pay room and board now that she is earning money. Her dream of independence suddenly vanishes. Inside, she is angry, even though she knows she has a duty to her family. She gives the money to her parents.

Sheri is looking for some way out of all her frustrations when she meets Tom, the strong and quiet type. He enjoys just sitting with Sheri and talking. Sheri never tells her parents about Tom because she fears that they will interfere with her relationship.

Tom is twenty-six and lives with some other fellows in an apartment close to the coffee shop. He works from four to midnight in the local welding shop. He always has lunch at the coffee shop and when she gets off work at two, they spend time together, usually at Tom's apartment. Ultimately, they become sexually involved.

Sheri becomes suspiciously aware of a change in her bodily functions and fearfully visits a doctor who confirms her suspicions. She's pregnant. Now she faces a new crisis. To whom can she turn? First she tells Tom, who takes responsibility for her condition and suggests that they immediately get married. However, as he thinks aloud, he begins to reconsider the alternatives. Maybe marriage isn't the answer. They aren't ready for that kind of a commitment. Perhaps an abortion is the best alternative. Sheri is devastated by the thought of an abortion and is forced into an extreme crisis.

When Tom goes to work, Sheri goes home. Seeing her despondency, Sheri's mother asks if something is wrong. Sheri answers that there is indeed something wrong, but that she is handling it just fine. Afraid to pursue the subject, her mother goes back to preparing dinner, which the family eats in awkward silence.

Still in turmoil, Sheri calls Kathi and pours out the whole situation. Kathi listens attentively and then invites Sheri to come over the next evening and visit with her and Art so they can consider some options together.

Meanwhile, at work the next day, Sheri remembers that Linda, another waitress, has had an abortion. Linda invites Sheri to her apartment and listens to Sheri's plight. Linda shares her experience with Sheri and reveals her own struggles. At the time of the abortion she had no problems, but now she often wonders what the child would have been like. She often feels guilty when she sees other babies and young children. "I'm quite sure that I wouldn't have another abortion," she adds. Because Linda listens and shares her own feelings, Sheri feels she has found a real friend.

Later Linda tells her where she can get an abortion, should she decide to go that route. She also tells Sheri about a group which provides counseling and help for women facing an unplanned pregnancy.

That evening Kathi and Art are very supportive as Sheri's options are discussed. Their first question is whether or not Tom is willing to get married. Sheri really isn't sure what Tom would say at this point. Kathi offers to go with Sheri to talk with Tom, but Sheri decides she and Tom need to make a decision without any outside pressure.

Saturday Tom and Sheri have the whole afternoon to talk. Out of heavy feelings of guilt, Tom agrees to marry Sheri, even though he is not in love with her. He makes it clear that his decision is made out of a feeling of responsibility, not from a desire to spend the rest of his life with her.

Kathi and Art accompany them to a neighboring state to witness the marriage and to lend support. When they return home, they all go to the parents' house to share the news of the marriage but not the pregnancy. Both parents are shocked and demand to know why Sheri made such a hasty decision. They are obviously suspicious, but, not wanting to deal with the issue, they grudgingly give their blessing and drop the subject.

Sheri and Tom move in with Kathi and Art until they can afford their own apartment. Within the year their baby girl arrives, and Sheri feels content with her decision not to have an abortion. Shortly after the baby is born, however, Tom and Sheri separate and eventually divorce. In time Sheri remarries. Her second marriage is working well, and Sheri's first child is well accepted by her new father. Although Sheri does see her parents occasionally, there's never been a real reconciliation. The family ties have never been restored.

Discussion

Sheri is typical of so many young women who become pregnant before marriage. Her crisis became complex because there were many factors and relationships with which to deal. First, Sheri had a substantial degree of rejection. She was rejected by parents, friends, society, co-workers, and some churches. People appear to have trouble making a distinction between rejecting the unacceptable behavior and accepting and loving the person.

Women confronted with an unplanned pregnancy have to deal with a decision involving another life.[7] In this book we cannot solve the issue of abortion. While we are opposed to abortion except when the life of the mother is in real danger, we realize that we do not have to make the decision, nor do we have to live with the consequences. We can be caring about a woman who decides to have an abortion, even though we disagree with terminating the life of an unborn child. To reject the woman who has an abortion is to compound an already difficult situation.

Women who have children out of wedlock or are married because of premarital pregnancy often become angry when they are forced to change their lives because of an unwanted child. The anger, hurt, and guilt may get transferred onto the developing child. Children born in a crisis often suffer over the years because of the crisis.

Frequently the mother is confronted with economic problems. How is she going to take care of the child? Can she continue her job? If not, where will she get money to take care of herself until the child arrives? Once the child arrives how is she going to pay the medical bills? As financial problems develop, emotional crises begin to compound.[8]

The father of the child is confronted with major decisions. Will he marry the mother, help pay for the pregnancy and support the child, deny being the father, run and hide, or attempt to put pressure on the mother to get an abortion? No matter which decision he makes, the father will have to deal with his feelings and the reaction of others to him. He will also need to deal with his responsibility for the child and his reaction to that responsibility. When helping someone who is going through the crisis, be sure to express concern to the father. He, also, may have tremendous need for support.

Parents of the mother- and father-to-be will be confronted with a crisis of their own. Some will wonder what they did wrong in raising their children; some will deny responsibility; others will assume all of the responsibility. In dealing with their crisis, they may overlook the crisis of the parents-to-be and the developing child. Issues and emotions of the parents' own premarital or extramarital sexual activity may come into sharp focus, resulting in an additional factor.

Friends and acquaintances of the parents-to-be will also react and influence the crisis. Often the parents-to-be will turn to friends or even recent acquaintances—being afraid to go to family or close friends for fear of rejection. Friends and acquaintances who give advice are influenced by their own values surrounding pregnancy and related issues.

Reaction of medical and other professionals sometimes has a bearing on how the couple in crisis deal with their problems. Cold and indifferent professionals do much damage. Those who are flippant or judgmental do much to compound an already tough problem. Professionals and institutions have a great potential for help. They need to be good listeners and solid sources of information.

Finally, churches, and particularly clergy, have a vital role in dealing with the crisis of premarital or extramarital pregnancy. A caring, sensitive, and patient pastor can be one of the most significant helpers in this difficult crisis. Some pastors are limited in what they can do, possibly because of the lack of training or because of limits placed on them by their congregations or denominations.

A counselor should notice these six points, vital to an effective ministry:

1. Be aware of your own feelings and values.
2. Avoid being judgmental. Nearly all people facing this crisis already feel guilty.
3. Focus on plans for the future rather than on past behaviors.
4. Be an active listener and notice the underlying emotions as they are expressed.
5. Let the persons involved know you sincerely care about them.
6. Help the people get professional medical care, and social services.

It is critical that we all learn to face this crisis with concern, love, and gentleness. One would hope this crisis will reduce in frequency as people recognize the depth of their personal responsibility when it comes to sexual activities. Each person going through this crisis can find reassurance and forgiveness (1 John 1:9), knowing that nothing can separate us from the love of God (Rom. 8:33–39).

Common Feelings and Issues for Counselors to Address

- overwhelming bewilderment caused by complexity of options and the importance of numerous decisions
- guilt as sins are made public
- blame of self or resentment toward men
- fear of rejection from parents, boyfriend, friends, church family
- confusion over identity as youth or mother
- decision to marry or not to marry (assessment of relationship)
- decision to keep or give up child
- concerns relative to financial support
- concerns regarding child care
- family members who feel shared guilt
- parents who feel they failed as parents

- baby's father overwhelmed by responsibility
- baby's father—similar feelings and issues as mother

Physical Abuse or Assault Victim

Case Example—Family Violence

Diane and Martin have been married for fourteen years. Early on, their marriage went fairly well. The kids started coming and life soon settled into a routine. Martin drove a delivery route and seemed pleased with his job. He was not advancing, but he liked seeing his customers, and liked getting off by 3:30 in the afternoon.

However, in the past few years dark storm clouds have been forming over their marriage. When he gets off from work, he usually stops by the bar for a couple of drinks. As she looks back over the past five years Diane admits that there has been a gradual increase in his drinking. When he would come home, there would be fights about his missing dinner and there never being enough money for all the needs of the kids. At times he would explode. The verbal fights would deteriorate into shoving and lately they'd been more frequent and violent. Diane would try to cover the black and blue spots with clothes or make-up, but emotions are never so easily hidden. The day after a fight Martin would be remorseful; he'd feel guilty and sorry for his behavior. He'd promise not to hit her again, but a few weeks later there would be more fights.

Diane comes to me after a severe fight. This time, their twelve-year-old son tried to interfere. Martin shoved the boy over a chair and he was hurt in the process. Diane accused Martin of being a child abuser, and that had prompted the most severe beating she had ever received. Now she has to do something; she sees no alternative.

Case Example—Assault

Cathy is a middle-aged woman who's never been considered beautiful. She is walking to her car in the shopping center parking lot when a man grabs her. He forces her to a dark corner of the lot, saying, "If you yell, I'll kill you."

Cathy is terrified. She prays that this crazy man will not kill her. He rapes her, hits her, and calls her names. He rapes her again. After what seems like an eternity, he leaves her. At first she feels lucky just to be alive.

Cathy lies where he left her, sobbing. No one comes to her rescue. She gets up and hastily dresses herself. She goes to her car and automatically starts to drive home. What is she going to tell her husband? What will he think? How will he react? Can she hide this from her children? *Should* she hide this from her children? Will she be blamed as if it were her fault? Why did this happen to *her?* These and other thoughts race through her mind. Then the full impact of all that has happened hits her. She feels dirty, defiled, used. Rage begins to build, yet she is confused.

Discussion

Few people have the coping skills necessary to handle the crisis produced by physical violence or assault. The violation of a person's body is an intrusion on his or her very personhood. The victim's freedom and primitive need for security are both threatened.

In the case of family violence, the crisis is complicated by the emotional complexities. Like Diane, most family members really love the abusive person. They feel a sense of betrayal mixed with concern for the person.[9] Where there is a physical assault or rape by an unknown assailant, the victim is much more free to be openly angry without the complexities created by an emotional bond.

Within violent families, victims often resist reporting the crisis situation because they don't want to betray someone they love by discussing or reporting the violence. They wonder if they have encouraged the violence by their arguments. They may not feel victimized as they may feel they deserved the abuse. Frequently, however, they are internalizing rage at being so violated.

Many wives feel helpless and assume their lives are out of their control. If they should leave their husbands, how could they ever support themselves or care for their children?[10]

Where would they live? What does the Bible say about separation?

Along with the helplessness comes the feeling of being trapped. They want a family life, yet this is so painful. But how can they leave? The crisis is often complicated by the poor self-concept that is derived by the victim who, over a period of time, may grow to resent herself. Children are particularly vulnerable.

In the case of family violence, the family is in crisis. Both the victim and the abuser are in need of crisis intervention. The abusing husband can learn alternatives to his aggressive behavior.[11] The abusing parent can be supplied with a friend who helps ease the burden and gives some social control and attention.[12]

Those who are in crisis due to assault or rape by an unknown person experience a related, but different, phenomenon. They may feel a more open anger, yet uncertainty about dealing with the social system. They may be hesitant to seek medical help or to make reports to the police. Will the helping professionals understand, or will they blame the victim?[13] Will the situation take months or years to resolve if it gets into the court system?

Victims may tend to be angry with God and ask, "Why me? Why did God let this happen to me? I didn't deserve this."

When a married woman is sexually assaulted, she may have concerns about her relationship with her husband. With this crisis, he may also need the opportunity to discuss his feelings, since their private, intimate relationship has now been violated.[14] At times, a rape may impact a couple's pattern of relating. Does the spouse and/or the victim feel the sexual relationship can never be the same again?

Healing from assaults may take years. In some cases, the person will not fully heal emotionally. Healing can be increased if the victim ultimately forgives the assaulter and any persons who let the victim down during the crisis.

No one needs to remain a victim. Each person can take responsibility for the rest of his or her life after the assault and find a new, effective life in spite of the tragedy of the past.

Common Feelings and Issues for Counselors to Address

- anger at being victimized
- grief over being violated
- loss of control over life
- loss of security
- concern for being blamed by others
- feeling wronged
- fear of being treated unjustly by justice system
- anger with God
- guilt for reporting family member
- lowered self-concept or negative self-image
- concern for sexual responsiveness with spouse

EMOTIONAL PROBLEMS

Case Example

Connie is a school teacher; her husband, Tom, has been a salesman for several years and is now a manager of an office supplies store. Sales are down, and Tom's company is undergoing a change in management. Tom has been coming home depressed, which is unusual for him. When Connie asks him what is wrong, Tom explodes. No one cares about him at the company anymore. They just don't understand that his accounts are down due to a slump in the economy.

The next morning Tom is very quiet, still depressed. Connie is getting worried because Tom is increasingly not himself. In the afternoon just as she is about to leave school she gets a phone call from Tom's employer who tells her that Tom is staring off into space and refuses to talk to anyone. She races to the office to discover that Tom has had a "nervous breakdown." Apparently, he had just heard through the grapevine that his job is in jeopardy because he has lost two of the company's biggest accounts.

Connie, along with one of Tom's coworkers, takes him to the psychiatric hospital where Tom will be admitted. After his admission she is told that the doctor can see her in the evening. They tell her that Tom is resting and it would be best to visit with the doctor before seeing Tom. Reluctantly, she leaves the hospital.

As she drives home, a multitude of thoughts begin to race through her mind. Will this be the last straw and will Tom really lose his job? How long will he be in the hospital? What will other people think? Will he be able to get another job after being in a psychiatric hospital? What will the children think? How should she tell them? What will people at the church think? How should she relate to him? These and many questions become subjects of concern in the developing crisis in Connie's life.

When Connie gets home she finds herself trembling. She gets a neighbor to watch the children. She needs to talk to someone, but whom? She calls her pastor at the church, but the office is closed. She attempts to reach him at home only to learn that he is visiting with another family. Connie can't wait for the pastor so she calls a friend from school. For over an hour they talk about what has happened. Suddenly Connie starts crying, and she begins to wonder what others will think of her.

She can't eat any dinner and just as she is ready to go to the hospital, the pastor calls. After a brief discussion, he volunteers to meet her at the hospital, and she is relieved she won't have to face Tom alone.

Connie and the pastor arrive about the same time. She reaches out toward him and he gives her a warm and reassuring hug. After a few minutes they are ushered into an office where Dr. Greene explains his assessment: Tom's emotional problem has been developing for some time.

Connie wants to know if she could have caused the problem.

Dr. Greene says that all of Tom's environment and relationships have had an impact on him. But the doctor doesn't know to what degree any specific factor has affected Tom. She says that Tom will need to be on medication and in the hospital for at least ten days. The entire family will need to be in therapy to help Tom. Dr. Greene is not too encouraging as to how long it will be before Tom can return to work.

Connie is upset—and even more so after she sees Tom. He is not himself. He is confused and doesn't make a lot of sense.

She wonders if he will ever be himself again. As she and the pastor leave, Connie breaks into sobs. *What do I do now?* she wonders.

Discussion

Most emotional problems develop slowly over a long period of time, but they create a crisis for the person and family at the point of breakdown. The exception to this is situational stress reaction, often called a "nervous breakdown," which may be caused in part by a person's perception of his or her world. Part of a person's emotional health is dependent on how well he or she perceives his or her ability to deal with given problems. Stress certainly increases as the frequency of one's perceived failures increases. As people fail to cope, they tend to spiral downward. Failure breeds dysfunctional (ineffective) behavior until some people drift from what is considered normal to abnormal behavior. They may withdraw from the real world into a more comfortable world of fantasy.

In considering how emotional problems develop, it is important to keep in mind that families do work as a system. Dr. Murray Bowen has done some outstanding research on the role of families in the development of certain emotional problems. His view is that pressure in the system, even from former generations, may be expressed by one family member. Emotional problems may also be impacted by interpersonal relationships outside the family. Work and social relationships frequently have an impact on the way people function. As people begin to be more successful in interpersonal relationships and less isolated they tend to have fewer emotional problems apart from family system stress. It is true that certain internal problems inhibit our resolution of current problems. Many of these internal problems spring from ineffective personal relationships stemming from childhood.

Even today there is a stigma associated with mental illness. No one wants to be labeled as "crazy," yet that's what our society does all too often.[15] The view of society in general needs to be addressed because it does impact families who have to deal with emotional breakdowns.

Let us deal with some basic facts.

1. Mental illness is not contagious. It is true that some contagious diseases can have a damaging impact on the central nervous system, but psychological problems are not transmitted like a cold. One need not fear contracting a problem when living with or working with those experiencing psychological distress.

2. Racial and social status by themselves do not cause emotional problems.

3. People who have emotional problems are not demon possessed.

4. The person who has an emotional problem most likely did not develop it over a single problem. As a consequence of sin in a person's life, emotional problems may develop, and certain sin problems may be manifestations of emotional problems.

5. Emotional problems are not inherited. If a parent has had an emotional breakdown, it does not mean the children will inherit this trait. Scientists are studying the evidence for physiologic factors and chemical imbalances as the etiology of psychosis, but, at present, there is no clear evidence that psychosis is inherited nor that the predisposition is inherited.

6. Ignoring or humoring the person facing the emotional problem will not make the problem go away.

Some families have a secret: One of them has been confined in a hospital for a psychiatric condition. What a tragedy that people feel shameful or unclean or unspiritual because they have a family member in a psychiatric hospital. Quite the contrary should be true. There would be something to be embarrassed about if a family member needed help and was not getting it. Concerned families need to be reassured of acceptance and given guidance concerning the telling of other family members and friends.

There are several issues to keep in mind when working with families who are adjusting to having a member placed in a psychiatric hospital. Family members may need to discuss how to relate to their loved one when they visit him or her in the hospital. They may also need help in knowing how to readjust at home since the hospitalized family member filled a unique role within the family. Another frequent concern has to do with recovery. Will the patient ever be his/her old self again, is a frequent question. With modern techniques and medication there is usually room to hope for good recovery, although this may be best answered by the patient's doctor.

Many people, sensing emotional problems stirring up within them, are afraid to seek help because they fear what others might think of them. Others just do not understand what is happening to them. In either case, people often need encouragement from others before they will seek help. Yet each person needs to understand that problems can get worse if he or she delays getting help and each individual needs to take responsibility for seeking his or her own help.

If you are dealing with a person who is psychotic, you will want to help his or her family gain assistance from qualified professionals. This needs to be done immediately, especially if he or she is potentially dangerous to self or others. We will address the issue of treatment and referral more specifically in Part III.

Common Feelings and Issues for Counselors to Address

- embarrassment of family members
- changes in family as result of hospitalization
- fear of unknown aspects of mental illness, patient's personality and behavior
- concern for knowing how to relate to patient
- possible unemployment and future employability
- questions of how to tell family and friends
- concern that family member will be seen as unspiritual
- uncertainty in relating to hospital staff and rules[16]
- loss of social status and esteem
- anxiety relative to unknown future

CHAPTER FOUR

PEOPLE CRISES

THE CRISIS INVOLVED WITH the loss or gain of other human beings is the most intensive of all types of crises. In this chapter, we will focus on people loss while recognizing that the gaining of a new relationship can also create a crisis. Because new relationships usually become "significant" over a period of time and are under the control of the people involved, they will be discussed in chapter 5. This chapter will deal primarily with people loss, which often happens suddenly and lacks the element of control so important to our equilibrium.

DEATH

Case Example—The Threat of Your Own Death

Mae is approaching her sixtieth birthday. Several weeks ago she was informed by her doctor that she has a type of cancer that is normally terminal; she might live for another two or three months. Mae took the most frequent and probably wisest course of action; she went to two other doctors to get more opinions. She was hopeful that the diagnosis was wrong, that the lab tests had been mixed up or some other mistake had been made. When the other doctors confirmed the diagnosis and the stage, Mae was not yet willing to give up. She had heard of people in her condition suddenly going into remission. Perhaps if she prayed, the Lord might reverse the disease. But just asking the Lord was not enough. She felt she needed to offer something to God. She would give the rest of her life to the Lord in some ministry. With a new-found fervor she prayed several times a day. Yet God did not seem to answer her prayer the way she wanted him to answer. As her condition worsened, she began to question if God were listening to her. Didn't Jesus say that anything could be done in his name? Perhaps she was not offering enough. She offered to give God whatever he wanted; still her condition declined.

Now she is asking more questions. Should she go to a minister who is successful in healing people? Could she go to another country where there may be another cure? On the other hand, maybe her problem is a wrong frame of mind. Possibly a diet change is what she needs. Mae goes through a long list of possibilities and continues to bargain until she becomes angry and wants to yell at God.

Case Example—The Death of a Loved One

I was in the military hospital as duty officer when a woman came in. She'd been told that her husband had been injured during a field exercise, but before she arrived he had died. The doctor in the emergency room had to break the news. In the seclusion of a small room he told her what had happened. The hall was soon filled with her screams of disbelief. "No, no! It can't be him!" The desire to disbelieve was there, but her sobbing and screaming indicated that she also did believe. This was only the beginning of the crisis. The doctor allowed her friends to be with her while she grieved. She could not believe that that morning's good-bye kiss had been the last. The day had started in such a routine way.

I didn't expect this woman to get much sleep that night, and I could just imagine the trauma of trying to make so many decisions the next day. She would have a difficult time, but she began working through the crisis even as she called other relatives to discuss with them all the details of what had happened.

Discussion

Like Mae, people who are dying go through different stages of feeling. These may include denial, bargaining, anger, depression, and finally acceptance or resolution, as suggested by Dr. Elisabeth Kübler-Ross.[1] Some people get stuck in a stage or will go back and forth between stages, but many people who have long-term illnesses leading to death finally accept their terminal conditions even with anticipation. This grieving process can be confusing and upsetting to both the patient and family members if they don't know what to expect.[2]

People deny reality when they're not ready to handle it or when they don't want to deal with it.[3] Often denial works to their benefit for a while. Some research suggests that individuals who deny their terminal illnesses will live longer than those who totally accept them. Normally, denial lasts long enough for the patient to adjust to the shock of being in a terminal condition.

Frequently, bargaining begins to emerge as denial is phased out of the consciousness of the dying person. Bargaining is based on the hope that by making some change the ultimate conclusion will not take place.

Similar to Mae, most people who are in a terminal condition try to find something they can do to change things. They feel they ultimately can control their environment. There is a great deal of truth to that idea, yet many times they have *no* control over their conditions. Their only alternative then is to change their view of what they are facing. The attempt to bargain may not be the best use of one's time; yet each person processes life experiences at his or her own pace.

Once a patient has accepted the reality of pending death, planning for the remaining days can begin—even though there will be limitations based upon the nature and state of the person's physical condition.

Normally, dying people deal with anger and/or depression after going through denial and bargaining stages. Once they realize that they are not going to get better, they often get angry over the "unfairness" of death at this time. Sometimes people will aim their anger at relatives, friends, or coworkers. Patients may go so far as to blame the person with whom they are angry for being the cause of the terminal disease. Harsh and shattering words may be exchanged. This may be a way for the dying persons to separate themselves from loved ones.

Anger may be directed toward God. Patients will sometimes hold in their rage, but they will let it build until they eventually deal with it openly. Many pastors and counselors have been faced with the issue of a dying person's anger with God. Tip-offs include, "God is being unfair to me," and "What did I ever do to deserve this?" In extreme cases patients have even been known to curse God over their conditions.

Generally the anger aimed at God or at others produces guilt within the patient. This guilt can produce further anger or even depression. Some Christians who have experienced this anger have felt they have lost their salvation. The sensitive pastor or counselor can remind the Christian patient of God's love and his understanding of what is going on in the life of the patient. Most Christians can recall that they are forgiven for their sins if they confess them to the Lord (1 John 1:9). Continuing guilt can result in a person getting emotionally stuck at this level and not being able to complete the adjustment task.

Depression in most dying patients is a result of a sense of loss. They are saddened over the impending separation from loved ones and possibly the interruption of work toward life goals.[4] It is difficult to say good-bye. Deep depression can develop over the loss of control of the life process and the futility of the battle. For non-Christians this depression may be deeper because they do not share the hope of a glorious eternal life. Christians can find great assurance in the words of the Lord:

> Let not your heart be troubled; you believe in God, believe also in Me. In My Father's house are many mansions; if it were not so, I would have told you. I go to prepare a

> place for you. And if I go and prepare a place for you, I will come again and receive you to Myself; that where I am, there you may be also. (John 14:1–3)

This is very real hope for the Christian. He or she can be assured of a future life in which there will be no more tears or suffering.

Many terminally ill patients are able to overcome depression by setting realistically specific short-term goals. As they are able to bring about a warm closure they can feel successful and worthwhile. Many patients settle old scores in a positive way. They write letters or call people they have not talked with in a long time. They write letters to children or grandchildren who are too young to know them well.

Some terminally ill patients are in settings where they can help others facing a similar problem. Patients may work with their hands, share experiences, or comfort someone else. We all need to feel of value to others. These patients, by helping, have found a sound method for defeating depression.

Overcoming the depression that precedes death requires that the patient do one small thing at a time. The knowledge of a small task completed gives a sense of value. There is also a real need for hope that can be found in a legacy left behind.

Many terminally ill patients go through the five stages we've discussed: denial, bargaining, anger, depression, and resolution. The last of these frequently becomes apparent in the final weeks of the dying process. Reconciliation comes about when the patient totally accepts the reality of his or her pending death and may even anticipate that time. This reaction is not merely the desire to avoid further pain; it is the reality of the conclusion. For the Christian, death itself is the beginning of a new reality with God.

Most pastors can recount a number of experiences with dying persons who have had an amazing peace as they faced death. Most of these people have not only accepted their pending death, but have looked forward to being with the Lord and with Christian family and friends. The reconciliation stage is furthered when family and friends also accept the death of the loved one and complete unfinished business (emotional closure) with the patient.

When the final hours of life can be filled with love, caring, and completion, the family carries away a peace that comes from knowing that they helped make the loved one's departure meaningful.

Families dealing with crisis associated with death often have difficulty accepting the loss of the loved one. One way the pain can be managed well is by sharing good, even humorous, memories associated with the loved one.

It is important for families to accept the relief they might experience after the death if they have been providing primary care for the patient. There is something special about helping a dying family member, yet there are burdens associated with caring. It is normal to feel some relief that the burden has been reduced—as well as some guilt for feeling that relief.

Most family members know that they can and should grieve. Allowing grief to take its natural course helps prevent complications that might come about if the feelings were squelched. Some people may need professional help if they get stuck in the grief process.

When a sudden and unexpected death occurs, the family dynamics may be slightly different.[5] The impact from the sudden death is somewhat alleviated by the busyness of the first few days. The arrival of relatives with their tremendous support is only the beginning of an adjustment process. The crisis is not yet over. People do not know what to say to someone in this situation. Reassuring platitudes are not nearly as important as just being there and being willing to listen. Those in this crisis may spend a great deal of time talking about the deceased. All of the tiny details of the day or days just before the death become suddenly important. Like sand that is sifted over and over through a screen, the details are sifted and resifted. So often people with good intentions have tried to think of the right words to say, have tried to be supportive, tried to ease the pain, but they are met with polite hostility and their comments fall on deaf ears. People going through sudden loss generally do not want to hear how "all things work together for good." They only feel that you don't understand their deep sorrow. They do not want to be told all of the advantages of not having to suffer long illness in old age. They feel that you are minimizing their situation. Their greatest need is for you to be with them. People are not always at a point where they can accept reassurance even when it is a truth.[6]

I recall friends who suddenly lost a child. The father told me later how much he had valued people just being there. Although he was a dedicated Christian he did not want all the Christian platitudes. This only fed his anger at the loss of his son. Some weeks later he finally admitted to God how angry he was at him. The father intellectually knew about God's divine providence and his ultimate goodness, yet he was honest enough to realize that emotionally he felt very differently toward God. His openness eventually led him to deal with his feelings toward God and allowed him to better accept what had happened. I say *better* because in some ways it appears to me that people who lose a young child never fully recover. The loss is so great that the scar tissue remains.[7]

The intense grief will subside as the one in crisis receives the support of others and works through the process of adaptation to the point of acceptance. It is not unusual for the person, however, to experience symptoms of loss of sleep, loss of appetite, and outbursts of anger. The anger may be directed at oneself or at others—for not doing more. You need not feel that you must be overly reassuring at these times. It is important for you to be realistic and point out the reality, while not being overly solicitous; this anger is part of the process of loss and not generally cause for concern.

Once the crisis has passed there still will be days of flashback loss. Holidays, birthdays, and anniversaries are times when the loss is felt again. Remember the need for support during these "special" days. Your job is not over when the immediate grief has passed. A person who has experienced sudden loss needs the counselor to help him or her prepare for holidays and special days. This principle is particularly true the first year, the first Christmas, the first birthday, and so forth. After each passing year it should become easier and easier. As years go by, the history of the mourner is filled in with new content. If every Christmas morning of her adult life Debbie opened presents with her husband, she has no other Christmas expectations. However, if after a few years she develops a new history or pattern which she can repeat and anticipate, the earlier pain begins to diminish.

The best medicine for the loss of a significant person may well be the formation of other significant relationships. However, do not push someone who has lost a significant person into new relationships until that person is ready. You may feel that one needs new relationships. But because you are not dealing with the same pain of loss, you may tend to push or encourage too soon. A person is not ready for a new relationship until there has been resolution of the former relationship. This is a process that takes months to achieve.

Following a significant loss, some reactions are not healthy and indicate a need for support. After years of marriage, one widow moved quickly back to life as usual. Within a couple of weeks of her husband's funeral she was dating again. She allowed no time for grieving, as if she'd buried all her feelings along with her husband.

But there are other red flags. Some people get very busy as if they are running from their feelings. Frequently such a person gets busy with so many activities that he or she gives no thought to the purpose or goal for the action. After thirty years of marriage another widow buried herself in feverish activity for six months after her husband's funeral. Only then did she slow down and allow herself to grieve.

Other people go into a state of withdrawal. They need someone to keep knocking gently on their emotional shells and inviting them out. This is their agenda: "I got deeply involved. I got hurt. I don't ever want that kind of pain again, so I won't get involved with anyone else—on any level." The price tag for safety is loneliness. Some may choose this route, but it is not possible for a Christian to continue to be part of the body of Christ and be isolated. The biblical goals of loving one another, bearing each other's burdens, being of one spirit, and being an integral part of the body become impossible to obtain, somewhat like a foot that tries to operate by itself. We can understand the fear of pain that can lead to this isolation, but such hurting people will need encouragement to step out of their four walls.

Others handle the process in a similar way by drinking or other numbing techniques. All of these responses should be taken as cries for help, not just symptoms to be judged and condemned.

What about children who have lost a loved one? Crises are not just for adults. Children also have them. We encourage extensive support. The child should have the opportunity to attend the funeral as long as he or she is past infancy and can verbally interact with adults. Children are sometimes overprotected from death in our society. They need to have the opportunity to grieve, to ask questions, to receive answers, and to talk about their feelings.

The person who provides crisis counseling during the death in a family will find no two situations alike. The loss will always be great, but the situation and ways individuals deal with loss will vary in accordance with their personalities.

Common Feelings and Issues for Counselors to Address

- shock
- rejection
- emptiness
- pain of mourning
- anger at God
- denial, bargaining, anger, depression, resolution
- disorganization of life
- lack of control of one's life
- need for comfort
- need to discuss the loss repeatedly
- loss of appetite, loss of sleep
- need for time before one can accept the loss
- preparation for readjustment during special days

Divorce

Case Example

A few months ago Mike came walking into my office. He was visibly shaken yet trying to control himself. He did not have an appointment but wondered if he could talk to someone. Since I had only about twenty minutes before I had to leave, I established that as the parameter for our time together.

The words and feelings were tumbling out faster than he would usually have expressed them. His wife had gotten a restraining order and he was moved out. Their relationship had been deteriorating for several years. The tensions had built and built. Last week he had become violent and threatened her. For several years he had ignored her pleas for his becoming more cooperative and involved in the family. His outburst of temper had increased the tension. She had a man friend whom she saw frequently. She felt he understood her. Mike had also threatened him. Now she was filing for divorce and he felt as if his whole world were falling apart. Several days earlier in his desperation he had turned his fury on himself. He showed me his arms where large scabs crossed his veins. "I guess the Lord didn't want me to die after all," he said. As he talked about her leaving him, the tears flowed down across his face.

Both he and his wife professed to be Christians. Mike felt they could put their marriage back together if only she would listen to him. He was willing to come for counseling or to do whatever it took to reestablish the marriage. He emptied himself as much as he could in the twenty minutes, and I scheduled a time for him to come back when we could spend more time talking. There was immediate relief, but I had the uneasy feeling that the relief was only temporary. In the weeks that followed, he did work through his great sense of loss. The marriage problem had progressed so far that the wife did in fact file for divorce. He was clinging to a straw in the wind in hopes that she would be willing to be reconciled.

Discussion

Separation and divorce are unique forms of people loss.[8] The loss is not only one of companionship; this is a grapelike cluster of loss.

First, loss of the relationship does exist. The person in crisis is cut off.[9] However, things get complicated because the significant other is not really gone; he or she is still alive, simply not available for relationship. The picture is usually clouded by an intense anger. The person in crisis often is attempting to deal with the separation and with anger or even a desire to reject the spouse. The mixture of love/hate often contributes to the crisis and can result in vast behavior swings as seen in Mike who swung from begging for reconciliation to threats of violence. For some there is a strong sense of abandonment. They feel isolated and left behind all by themselves. Fear is very great as they think they cannot face the world alone.

Frequently, self-esteem is also lost. The person feels worthless and like a failure.[10] If a person feels not valued by another whose attentions are desired, that first person tends to devalue him- or herself. Some people in this crisis state expend considerable time berating themselves for all their mistakes or labeling themselves with degrading terms such as *total failure*. Christians also often carry a significant sense of guilt. They know they are making decisions or are being forced into a position in violation of church teachings. For some, this means dropping out of Christian circles during a time of great need for the ministry of the body of Christ.

Another concern is for the children and the impact that this will have on their lives.[11] Divorcing parents often feel a sense of guilt because of the effects on their children. One cannot deny that the children are going through strong emotional reactions and that they are experiencing intense feelings that need attention. Children may be blaming themselves for the separation even when that is not realistic.[12] They may be hurt by one parent's anger at the other or feel they have to choose sides. As a helping professional you will want to be aware of the needs of children during this crisis.

One or both of the spouses may need to resolve internal

anger. The lives of some people revolve around anger toward spouses. They may feel that they are victims of their spouses' whims. They may feel that unwanted separations have been forced on them. Sometimes a third person is involved which compounds the anger with rejection and jealousy. The loss of family, friends, and supportive others may also complicate matters. Family friends who don't want to choose sides, who do not know what to say, or who do not want to be involved may retreat. This may be especially true for those who are involved in church groups.

Divorce or separation often involves a change in roles. If children have left a person's care he or she may spend significantly less time in the role of parent. Of course the role of wife or husband has disintegrated. The divorced person may be asked to step down from a church role if, for example, he or she is on the elder board or is a Sunday school teacher. The loss of familiar roles generates a crisis within a crisis.

For many wives, separation or divorce brings a work overload. They are usually given custody of the children, and they may have to seek employment due to financial stress. Yet the laundry needs to be done, the kids are fighting, the car isn't running properly, and the lawn needs mowing but the mower won't start.

The church can and should be a resource. Although the church need not sanction divorce, it can facilitate a healing process when this crisis occurs.

Common Feelings and Issues for Counselors to Address

- loss of self-worth
- failure, rejection, and abandonment
- anger
- control of anger
- loss of companionship
- fear of being labeled and rejected by friends
- loss of roles
- guilt
- loss of supportive friends
- worry about effects on children

- overload of tasks and responsibilities
- financial crisis
- uncertainty of future

Moving

Case Example

She grew up in the Midwest but now lives in Los Angeles. Dora is bright, personable, and enjoys her family. Jack is an executive who carries a great deal of responsibility. Even so, his family is important to him and he is attentive to his wife's needs. She lives in an upper middle income neighborhood, but her friends are from a variety of backgrounds. She has several close friends with whom she feels she can share and often sees them in a Bible study group which has become a strong supportive group. But one by one over a period of a few years her friends move away. The loss of these friendships is very difficult for Dora, especially since she dislikes living in Los Angeles and dreams of someday returning to the Midwest. The group in which she is involved tends to be "upwardly mobile," and new and better jobs always seem to call the families elsewhere.

Kathy is a friend Dora has especially grown to love and treasure. Dora plunges into a state of depression the day Kathy comes to Bible study and shares the news that she, also, is to move away; her husband is being transferred. Dora tries to hide her depression and disappointment from Kathy because she wants to be happy for her, but the loss is intense for Dora. She feels abandoned in a foreign land. Los Angeles, never "home" to her, is tolerable because of Kathy's presence. Now she is leaving. Dora says, "I think I will never again make friends. Every time I finally develop a good friendship she moves away. I can't stand any more loss."

After a number of years of feeling abandoned and isolated, Dora herself experiences upward mobility. Her husband accepts a job offer that looks very promising and they are the ones who move away.

Discussion

Moving has become a prevalent form of people loss in our mobile society. Friends as well as family members move frequently.[13] Young people move away to school, middle-aged people move to different employment opportunities, older people move away to retirement spots. All of these moves uproot the relationships of those who move and of those who remain behind.

Part of the emotional impact on the person left behind may be the realization that the friend has chosen to move away. How does a person process being left behind? The person may feel abandoned, insignificant, or rejected. One person who was dealing with this issue recently asked, "Doesn't he care? Aren't I important to him?"

The person moving away may experience bittersweet feelings. The sadness of losing a friend or relative is felt, but so is the enthusiasm and anticipation of a new adventure. The ones left behind may have a hard time processing the loss when the "movers" excitedly explain that they feel this is God's leading in their lives.

On the other side of the picture is the crisis experienced by those who are moving away. The loss of friends and sometimes the loss of family is extensive.[14] They may never again see some ill or elderly people they are leaving behind. When those who are left behind are elderly parents, there may also be a sense of guilt in addition to the loss. Even when there are plans to see friends again, because of distance and time, the relationships will never be the same. Therein is the loss.[15]

For those moving, the issues are complex. First of all, does the whole family agree to the move? Teenage children will be losing peer relationships that are particularly valuable to them at their level of development. A family with children should plan, if at all possible, to move before or after their children have moved through the teen years. The husband and wife may disagree on where they should live. If one spouse is forced to move because of the other's career, resentment may become a part of the crisis. It's best if the whole family can plan for and agree upon the move together.[16] If singles are moving they do not have the complex issues of family, but they don't have others with whom to share the moving process either. This isolation may magnify the adjustment for them. Likewise, they may have no companionship in their new location. Loneliness can be especially strong for them at the point of settling into their new location.

In addition to the loss of friends, people who move sometimes settle into new communities where they have no initial emotional support. In all probability they don't even know where the stores are located or which doctor to go to. Just the unfamiliarity of the physical environment is stress producing.

I find this section easy to discuss since my family moved from California to Kansas a couple of years ago after living in the same community for eleven years. The loss of many friends and relatives was a major component to our crisis. But there were other losses. As we left the house and yard in which the kids had grown and played, we were aware of the many memories that had been formed there. No longer would we be a part of the place that linked us to so many events in our lives. As much as we anticipated going to a new community and job, we had a lot of questions and apprehensions about the unknown and unfamiliar. We would be strangers in a strange land. How would the new job work out? Would the new employer be difficult, unreasonable, or a complete joy? Would the people be friendly? Would a good church be nearby? Would the kids make friends and fit in?

Fortunately for us, we had friends in the community to which we moved. They gave us support, information, and resources, and introduced us to others. Having people you know in the new community can make an immense difference.

Common Feelings and Issues for Counselors to Address

Person left behind:

- abandonment and rejection
- conflict of joy for friend versus anger of loss
- loss of self-esteem or loss of personal value
- loneliness

Person moving:

- loss of friends
- apprehension about making new friends
- possible loss of control of life, if spouse decides on the move
- enormity of decisions
- vulnerability in unfamiliar environment
- uncertainty of new work environment
- loneliness in new community; lack of support network
- concern for children
- fear of unknown

Conflict with a Friend

Case Example

Their families have been friends for a couple of years. There have been some minor irritations but nothing major. Now Mrs. Baker is meeting with the pastor to discuss the situation since both families attend the church. She has been unable to sleep for the past few days and is obviously in distress. She keeps insisting that she does not want to say anything negative about the Davis family. After all, she knows she is not perfect either. But it is clear to the pastor that she does want to say something negative and that she has very little insight as to her part in the conflict which began over a disagreement between their children. Soon each mother was protecting her own child. One thing led to another and before long the accusations about many issues flowed. Mrs. Baker now is resigning from the women's missionary circle. She feels she can't work in the same group as Mrs. Davis. The hurt and bitterness are obvious. The pastor is concerned that both women might start aligning others to their sides and that things might get out of hand.

Discussion

Conflict with a close friend can cause a great feeling of loss. Although the dynamics are different, this loss has many similarities to other people-loss crises. Friendships vary a great deal in their depth and meaning so the crisis load can vary according to the friendship. The wife who cannot relate to her husband may be closer to an old female friend than to her own family. At the other end of the spectrum, some people may not be deeply involved in any one friendship. Time and the intensity of the relationship are both variables. The status of the friend may also be an issue. If the friend has high status, a person may derive a sense of self-worth from being associated and accepted by this friend. The friend's rejection, then, may weigh heavily on the person. In situations where friendships are less intense than family relationships, the crisis will be less severe than the loss of a family member.

Friendship loss is a unique situation. Because the crisis may exist as a result of a major disagreement, there is the possibility for repairing the relationship. This factor adds a different dimension from other people-loss crises. In the crisis that stems from death there is no hope for a recovery of relationship; when couples decide to divorce, the chasm between them is so deep and the relationship so intense that this possibility rarely exists.

The nonexclusive nature of friendship can decrease the loss reaction. By law a person can have only one spouse. In a divorce or in the death of a spouse, no back-up person absorbs the loss. But a person can have many friends and their presence can cushion the loss although the crisis will still be painful. One's childhood background can influence the level of stress one feels when losing a friend. One woman who grew up in a home where she assumed the responsibility for the whole family now feels guilt if any friend gets upset; she works hard at keeping everything in balance. The weight that she carries is incredible. A dispute that threatens her relationship with a friend would bring sleepless nights and loads of anxiety to her.

Friendships do need to be recognized as valuable, emotion-laden connections to others. They need to be treated with a sense of stewardship, so that those involved prevent them from easily breaking and causing trauma.

Common Feelings and Issues for Counselors to Address

- loss of support and acceptance; rejection
- anger

- self-doubt
- confusion as to who is right or wrong
- embarrassment about accusations
- guilt
- worry about being maligned
- worry about loss of mutual friends

CHAPTER FIVE

LIFE-CYCLE CRISES

SOLOMON SAID, "To everything there is a season, A time for every purpose under heaven: A time to be born, And a time to die" (Eccles. 3:1, 2).

This can provide the model for a consideration of life-span development. From early childhood to old age there are stages of change through which people move. At each stage, new, inexperienced, developmental tasks need successful resolution. Moving from stage to stage causes marked changes in people's lives. We would like to look at a few of these in anticipation of the stress issues that people will face at these different stages.

Because of space limitations, we will look at only selected

crisis points that occur in adulthood: marriage and remarriage, the birth of children, the impact of adolescence on the family, the empty-nest period, retirement, and aging. There are even more developmental tasks that we cannot mention within the confines of this book.

Built into the natural flow of life are many crisis points. A significant number of these have to do with marriage and family life. While we recognize that not everyone marries or has children, we feel that everyone is affected by family life. Single adults and childless couples also face crises around the issues of marriage and family. The decision to stay single, desiring marriage but not finding a suitable partner, deciding to remain childless, or discovering infertility—these create issues that influence the rest of life.

Recently a successful executive came to talk with me about how she was dealing with her recent birthday. She had been in college until her mid-twenties. During her early thirties she was building a dynamic career when she met a man whom she thoroughly enjoyed. They lived together for a time but never married. When he unexpectedly died, she needed a couple of years to recuperate. During her mid-thirties she dated many men and when she was nearly forty she found a man whom she wanted to marry. He, however, had children from a previous marriage and was adamantly opposed to having any more. Her life-long dream of raising a family was virtually gone and she felt forced into making a difficult decision: to marry this man or to look for someone with whom she could have a family. Time was pressing her and she was definitely in the midst of a crisis.

On the following pages we discuss the crisis of marriage and life-span development.

These life-cycle crises are somewhat different than some of the other crises. They usually are expected. People know certain events are coming but often do not realize that the events will cause major disruptions in their stabilized lives. Even those who anticipate emotional discomfort cannot go through the emotional experience and the adjustment until the event actually occurs.

Marriage

Case Example

A year ago, Candy lived with her parents who gave direction, bought the food, planned the meals, made the house payments, and cleaned the house. A few months ago Candy became Mark's bride. Now they make the decisions, plan the meals, budget the money. The external structure of their lives is gone. New roles and rules will be slowly worked into this new family. Adjustment will be the name of the game.

In her house Candy's father always took care of the car and the lawns. He left the cooking up to her mother. But one night Candy comes home and finds Mark fixing dinner. He is excited and is enjoying it. She is angry and feels pushed out of her territory. This is "her" job. Doesn't he like her cooking?

Mark always expected to keep the checkbook. His father made all the financial decisions in his family. But when he opens the checkbook to pay the bills, he discovers that she has written a forty-dollar check for clothes. Crisis number two has just arrived! And number three is soon to follow. He says, "You wrote out a check for clothes. I don't want you to do that."

She replies, "Who are you? My father? Since I work, I spend what I want."

One night Mark is late coming home from work because he wants to see a friend about car repair. When Mark gets home he finds his lovely and sweet bride is neither as lovely nor sweet as he thought. She is livid. She'd worried that he had been in an accident, *and* the dinner she knocked herself out preparing is ruined. He resists having to report in to his wife, as he had been forced to do with his mother.

Mark is like his father—quiet. His father talked when he had something to discuss, but never talked about his feelings. Candy comes home expecting her husband to share his day at work, just as she shares hers. But he feels there is nothing unusual to talk about, and besides, she can't understand all his technical jargon. From his point of view, there is nothing to tell her. Her disappointment grows as she feels that he is withholding himself. When she confronts him, he withdraws even more. In her family, a lively disagreement was considered healthy; in his family, issues and conflicts were avoided. They grew up with different concepts of communication.[1]

What a shock it is when you are attached to your parents and then suddenly move away. Right after she married, Candy talked to her mother every day. Her mother was a major source of encouragement and support. But she and Mark are thinking of moving to the West Coast. If they do move it would be at least two years before they return. Who would go shopping with her? Who would be supportive on days when nothing went right? She hopes Mark will fill the gap, but he'll never be her mother. That close relationship that she's enjoyed for twenty-two years is suddenly about to be interrupted.

Mark is also attached to his family. Candy has been after him for weeks to fix a dripping faucet. He promises to do it, but doesn't. He is always too busy. One Saturday morning his mother calls and wants her dishwasher fixed. He tells her he can postpone mowing the yard; he'll be right over. What happened? How can he do such a thing? Candy wonders if he loves her more than he loves his mother. Why can't he stand up to her and say, "No. I'm too busy to come right away"?

Candy and Mark eventually work their way through many issues. They adjust well to the crisis of marriage, but these same adjustment skills will be needed again and again as they face new challenges.

Discussion

A variety of factors can cause newlyweds to be in crisis. In some respects, the crisis of marriage can be positive. People are in love, on cloud nine. This in itself is an interruption to their emotional equilibriums. Some of the adjustments, however, are more painful.

Expectations are one part of the crisis. Most people look for spouses who will be all loving, all giving, and all sufficient. People come into marriages with intense hopes that their wishes and dreams will now become reality. Maybe a man's mother never paid attention to him. Now he thinks he will marry someone whose life will focus on him. Perhaps a woman's father was critical of her. Now she marries a "knight in shining armor" who has nothing but praise for her during courtship. Essentially, people expect their spouses to fill the gaps left by their parents. But three months after the lovely wedding, she gets interested in an activity with her girlfriend and ignores him. He criticizes her. Both parties quickly realize that the celestial being they married is only human. At this phase of realization "the honeymoon is over."

Newlyweds also need to adjust to new roles. She will have a definition of roles based on her family of origin and he will have a different set of role expectations based on his family of origin.

A couple also is quickly faced with learning that being involved with another person can affect one's personal freedom. They begin to see that their behavior affects the *two* of them. For two people to share a life, each must adjust to interrelating with the other. Each needs to have some knowledge of the spouse's behavior. Part of one's carefree, independent lifestyle needs to be modified. One hopes each spouse will view the adjustment as an exchange of independence for interdependence.

Communication is another factor that generates stress. It takes time and patience for a couple to share the meaning they equate with certain words, phrases, or actions.

Another aspect of the marriage crisis is the in-law pressure. Even the record of the genesis of humanity notes the in-law situation. Couples are encouraged to leave their families and also cleave to each other (Gen. 2:24). Often people aren't sure quite what to do with their in-laws other than to make jokes about them.

These facets added together lead all couples into a state of crisis shortly after marriage. One hopes this crisis becomes a means of growth. It takes a strong commitment for a couple to work through the crises that come during the first few years. Many couples don't get over this hurdle, and quickly divorce. Usually commitment stems from a couple's belief that two *can* become one and that two *can* stay together and work at the relationship when the stress is high.

Common Feelings and Issues for Counselors to Address

- loss of structure; adjustment to new structure
- emotional high

- disappointment from unfulfilled expectations
- adaptation to new roles
- loss of dependency on parents
- letting go of family of origin
- need for clarification of meanings in communication
- building relationships with in-laws
- moving from independence to interdependence

REMARRIAGE

Case Example

Bob has three children and Sandy has two. They feel sure that together they will be one big, happy "Brady Bunch." But soon after the marriage her kids start having trouble accepting Bob's authority. This is especially true of the older ones. He sometimes sides with his kids because he feels that Sandy is absolutely unfair with her demands. He and her older boy grow into more conflict every week, until her son leaves to go live with his own biological father. Bob's younger children feel that if they accept Sandy as "Mom," they will be disloyal to their own mother. They begin to resist merging as a family. There may be instant oatmeal and instant coffee, but there's no instant step-parent.

Before Bob's divorce, his daughter Ginny had been distressed about her mother's drinking problem and frequent absences from home. Sometimes Ginny would take her books and wait in the car while her mother was in a bar. Ginny could never seem to get her mother's attention. Following the divorce she looked forward to Bob's remarriage. Sandy seemed very nice, and Ginny just knew that Sandy would have all the time in the world for her. Ginny thought she would get the attention that she had always wanted. However, due to the tight finances, Sandy has to work. She tries to have some time for Ginny, but after she arrives home, prepares the meal, does the dishes and laundry, there is little time left. When Ginny begins losing interest at school and getting into arguments with the teacher, the family becomes more aware of the stress that Ginny is experiencing. Sandy tries to arrange her housework so the two of them can be together and spend time talking and sharing ideas and feelings.

The new family also faces logistical problems. There are now two mother figures, two father figures, and eight grandparents. The family faces the question: who spends time with whom? When and how do they get there? The family plans a party for grandfather's birthday. But it is also the weekend for Bob's kids to be with their mother and stepfather. To complicate matters, that Friday night Sandy's daughter has a piano recital and Saturday morning Bob's son has a baseball game. The birthday party has to be postponed. In large, blended families it takes a skilled administrator with a computer just to keep everyone's schedule straight and to make sure they get where they're supposed to be—on time.

Finances are also tight. Every month when Bob sends a check to his ex-wife, Sandy gets very irritable. But when her own child support check doesn't arrive, the whole household gets tense. There seem to be so many issues and such an overload that nobody seems to know what is going on in the family.

Discussion

The issue of remarriage raises some of the marital issues we previously discussed, as well as some new ones. Over one-half million adults remarry each year. At this time in our history, nearly one-half of all American marriages terminate in divorce, and about 75 percent of these people remarry, ofter assuming that life with the new partners will be very different than it was with their ex-spouses. This expectation leads into the first crisis—comparing the new husband with the ex-husband or the new wife with the ex-wife. Remarried couples tell us that although they try not to compare, their ex-spouses do become reference points. Many times they keep these feelings to themselves, but sometimes in the heat of the battle, feelings have a way of slipping out. Usually the spouse loses because his or her weaknesses are compared to selected strengths of the "ex."

The next crisis comes when ideas and dreams of a beautiful life together do not quickly come true. His kids and her kids usually end up mixing about as well as oil and water. The dream of one big happy family often ends up remaining just a dream rather than a reality.[2]

In addition to the adjustments to the new family, both the

children and parents are still processing the loss of their former situation. Recent studies have shown that most kids whose parents have been divorced for five years still carry a hope that their parents will remarry.[3] This applies even when both parents have remarried someone else and even when there has been physical violence in the family. Depending on the circumstances, the parents may also be dealing with fairly intense feelings of loss from their first marriages. For this reason, it is never a good idea to remarry until the person has nearly or completely worked through his or her feelings of loss. Most authorities think that this takes anywhere from a year to one-half the length of the original marriage.

In most cases, financial loss is another stress on the reconstituted family. This can trigger feelings from anxiety to resentment and hostility. In most states there are now fairly standard formulas for determining child support payments, but many divorced people feel the crisis of financial loss. Many husbands feel that they have been "taken to the cleaners." They renew their resentment each month when they send off the payment to the ex-spouse. Except for a few families where the wife had been a financially struggling single parent, the family simply must adjust to doing with less than they had before. It can be difficult to give up some of the new clothes, trips, sporting events, and restaurant dining. Pressure again sets into the family lifestyle.

If healthy patterns for coping with numerous and complex relationships do not develop quickly, unhealthy ones may disrupt the relationships for years. In a majority of remarriages, at least one partner already has children. Many have both "his" and "hers" and some have added "their" children.[4] There may be conflicts over who favors whose children, differences in style of discipline, subgroups forming in the new family, or children interjecting themselves as wedges between the new mother/father figure. The relationships with relatives, particularly grandparents, can be difficult, especially if the grandparents treat hers, his, and theirs differently.[5]

Schedules are usually hectic and mainstreaming communication is very difficult simply because of the number of people involved in decisions. One can understand why the rate of divorce is even higher in reconstituted families than it is in first-marriage families. There is a tremendous need for support in the blended family as it struggles through a whole series of minicrises.

Common Feelings and Issues for Counselors to Address

- adjustment to new relationship
- comparison with ex-spouse
- frustration at complexity of relationships
- discouraged when not instantly one big, happy family
- loss of relationships in ex-family
- financial pressures
- tension in relationships with extended family
- difficulty with numerous people's schedules
- tension around issues of fairness and discipline with children
- conflict and stepsibling rivalry

CHILDREN

Case Example

Mary and Tom are elated when they discover that Mary is expecting their first child. But as the months wear on, Mary begins to experience some ambivalent feelings; her school-girl figure disappears and she wonders if she is still attractive to Tom. Sara's birth into the family brings many moments of sheer delight, and even the sleepless nights do not dampen Tom and Mary's enthusiasm for this tiny addition. Many adjustments come as a new family schedule is instituted to accommodate the needs and desires of another member. But Mary, who had been neglected by her own father, often feels twinges of envy as Tom rushes home in the evening to talk and play with Sara, leaving Mary to do dishes and chores alone. Tom struggles with his own concerns of financially supporting a larger family, but both have the ability to focus positive attention and input into their home life.

Eventually they have a second and third child, and, by the time Sara enters adolescence, power struggles and rebellion occasionally disrupt a family that usually enjoys tranquillity. This new stage is a difficult time for the whole family as the children each demand freedom and push away from the authority of the parents. When Sara leaves for college, some of the dynamics of the family change since she has been the major focal point for the family. In time all the children launch into their own careers, and Tom and Mary look forward to the day when they will be grandparents.

Discussion—Birth

All parents will experience a series of crises as they raise their children. Usually the family is set off-balance when there is a birth, during adolescence, and as the children are launched. Even after the children have left home and are functioning as independent adults, their life circumstances may, at times, deeply affect their parents.

The birth of a child does not bring a couple together like a carefully designed weld, but rather introduces significant pressure on a marital relationship.[6] The intensity of crisis varies from person to person depending on the extent of change in relationships and the importance attached to that change by each person.[7]

For the mother, the delight of being pregnant may be counterbalanced by fear of the unknown. What will the birth and hospitalization be like? Perhaps she interprets the pregnancy as terminating her youthfulness. Certainly, the introduction of a third family member will shift the husband-wife relationship and roles. The change can be toward familial health and strength or toward dysfunction, depending upon how this birth-experience crisis is resolved.[8] Husband and wife have their lives neatly set up, have balanced their power structure, and have set in place a communication system. Then enters baby like an Oklahoma twister, and everything is out of kilter. They can no longer talk because baby is crying. The vocal one beckons as Mom and Dad sit down to dinner. There goes a nice quiet meal together. Every day the mail carrier brings a new pile of bills—anesthesiologist, photo studio, life insurance, pediatrician, the new stroller. The pressure builds until there is a family explosion which comes all too easily in the volatile environment of two frazzled and weary parents. When he comes home, why does Dad go to baby first? Why is the marriage relationship dull and not exciting? Does this mean that he doesn't love her as he used to? The triangle has started to form.

In the years to come patterns will continue to solidify. With good communication, a strong family will develop. With poor communication, a complex series of power plays, struggles, and manipulations will ensue—with one member of the triangle playing off against the others.[9]

Discussion—Adolescence

There are other crises, including little Sara starting school, getting injured, having her first tooth knocked out, or going to stay with Grandma and Grandpa for a few days. But the next routine crisis is that terrible, wonderful period when Sara becomes an adolescent. In some ways, adolescence reminds me of an old locomotive racing down the tracks when the engineer suddenly throws it into reverse. The wheels screech and sparks fly as it slides along the tracks and then slowly but surely begins rolling backward. Much of the family momentum has gone into growing up, building close ties, doing things together, gaining cooperation and obedience. Just as the family has gained steam and is finally moving well, everything screeches to a halt. Mom and Dad don't want Sara to be too grown up. Sara disagrees with everything they believe in. She wants to spend Saturday with her friends, not with the family at the stupid old zoo. Her room certainly does not reflect cooperation and cleanliness. She yells and screams and cries and ten minutes later shows up with matronly composure to enjoy an evening out with Mr. Mature who is all of sixteen.

Sara doesn't always understand what is happening either. All she knows is that her feelings run deep. Due to bodily chemical changes, adolescents experience great mood swings which they ride like someone in a small boat bobbing on an ocean. They get carried up and down by the waves. They want desperately to be grown-up, to be independent, and they need to be accepted by friends. Mom and Dad are from another era and don't know the latest musical group nor the slang of the day. Who wants to be associated with someone so out of it?

The issue of identity and "Who am I, anyway?" cuts across a number of areas of the parent–child relationship, but particularly in the aspects of freedom and power. If you are Sara and want to be accepted as such, you can no longer be known as the daughter of Mr. and Mrs. Jones. Therefore, you must push away and create distance and differences between yourself and your parents. You must become distinct. The best way to do that is to get your own ideas, express them frequently, and disagree at every available opportunity. Hence, Mom and Dad's ideas, which were mirrored in childhood, are no longer espoused. If Mom says it's white, Sara is absolutely sure that it is black.[10]

Discussion—Grown Kids

When parents get tired and think that their kids will never leave, lo and behold, they do. All the noise Mom thought would never end, stops. All of the food that ran through the refrigerator like water through a sieve, just sits there. Now lettuce begins to wilt, carrots grow limp, and apples grow soft—right on the refrigerator shelf. All of the time a mother never had for herself because she was a chauffeur, roller skate repairman, psychologist, or surgeon removing a splinter, begins to weigh on her. It's not just the noise and toys that are gone, it's also the excitement and expectation of something new happening every day. This means that new experiences have to be built into one's life so that some of the old void is filled. Imagine a mother who valued herself because she felt that she was a good mother. Where has all her worth gone? Suppose her identity was tied primarily to the kids. "I am Mother, and I do all of these motherly things—buying kids' clothes, cleaning out old banana peels from lunch boxes, and fixing gourmet hot dogs." Now when she stops these functions, who is she? It may be crisis time.[11]

Another change has to do with the husband–wife relationship. The kids started a crisis by entering the family system; now they create another one by leaving it. Husband and wife no longer have all the triangles to communicate around. They have each other—one to one. For some families this adjustment has been magnified by the wife getting lost in the kids and the husband getting lost in his job. The kids leave and Mom and Dad suddenly realize they are strangers despite the fact that for twenty years they have shared the same kitchen, the same bathroom, the same bed. They haven't talked or developed their relationship to any depth. They now need to learn to talk to each other or they will rapidly pull into their separate worlds, most likely never to establish their relationship again.

When the kids finally are grown and settled, the parents heave a sigh of relief and assume that the crisis with kids is over. They have done their jobs in launching them; now they can relax and sit back. No more crises . . . but then one hits. Junior is twenty-six, married, has two wonderful children, and is doing well in his job. The parents are proud and love to have them over for backyard barbecues. One evening he comes by the house. As he walks in the door they know that something is wrong. They ask what's wrong and anticipate something major. He tells them about the changes at work. The old administrators have been moved out by the parent company and the new boss is bringing in his own people. His world is shaken. Where will he go? What will he find to do? They talk, reassure, and remind him of his progress. They promise to loan him some money and to help whenever they can. Yet that night they do not sleep well. Their lives have also been affected. Although they had launched him eight years earlier, he is still their son. They are still emotionally engaged. His crisis becomes their crisis.[12] Old parental feelings of protectiveness are again stirred within. Emotionally, their equilibrium has been upset.

In one sense parenting never ends. We do not view this as a terrible fate. It may be good that families bind us so closely to each other. We encourage people not to expect the crises with kids to end once they have moved out of the nest. Children and grandchildren may return again for support during times of distress.

Common Feelings and Issues for Counselors to Address

New birth:

- excitement and joy
- physical exhaustion
- fear of unknown health of child
- stress from change in relationships
- adaptation to new parental roles
- loss of youthfulness and formation of new identity

Adolescence:

- dealing with independence and power struggles
- adaptation to rapid mood swings
- conflict
- letting go of child
- joy, pride in the child's achievements
- sadness and loss at launch

Adult children:

- distress at children's distress
- enjoyment of a relationship
- concern for well-being
- examination of and reflection on role as parent
- joy, pride at children's life success

Retirement and Aging

Case Example

She worries about him. He comes home tired and often falls asleep on the couch after dinner. His age is beginning to show, especially since his surgery three years ago. She can hardly wait until he is sixty-five. For the last two years, more and more of their conversation has been on what they would do when he retired. They anticipate catching up on their projects at home and then making a trip to Texas to visit their children and grandchildren. Retirement will be wonderful. The days roll by and soon the calendar is turned to *the* month. The big day is circled. The retirement party comes and is all that they had hoped for. The next day they enthusiastically start repainting the extra bedroom. The first week is fine, but by week two he is looking for things to do around the house. He begins to wonder what's going on at the office. He remembers some personal papers he left there. That's a good reason to stop by the office at coffee break time, but the next day he misses his friends more than ever. She begins to find him underfoot. She always went shopping Tuesday morning, but he wants her to help him paint shelves in the garage. He expects her to fix hot lunches. He is always asking for something and interrupting her schedule. They begin to pick at each other.

The trip to see the kids is wonderful. They even begin considering a move to Texas, but then they'd have to leave their home and all of their roots. Here they know the mechanic. They know of a good clothing store. They have a favorite bakery. The store clerks and bank tellers know them and speak to them. In Texas nobody would know them. They'd have to show I.D. cards at the banks to cash a check. They'd constantly get lost in the big city.

Down inside he begins to wonder who he is. He had always been a bookkeeper, but now he isn't. His solid identity suddenly has a big hole in it. He feels as if he has no value. They appreciated him at work. Now he isn't contributing anymore. He has a gnawing sense of uselessness and purposelessness. She tries to help by designing jobs around the house, but he only feels like her assistant. The crisis of retirement may well take a number of months to resolve.[13]

Discussion—Retirement

People go through several phases of trying to adapt to retirement. Those who adapt most successfully are those who planned meaningful relationships and purpose *before* retirement. The more families can absorb, encourage, and include parents who are retiring, the less difficult the crisis. The pressure points of changing routine, loss of peer groups, loss of identity, changes in the husband–wife relationship will all be there. Retirement is a mile marker. Some folks feel it signals the end of life; they sit in a rocking chair until death comes along as a relief from boredom. This does not have to be the case, as is so well illustrated by Mildred Vandenburg (author of *Fill Your Days with Life*), who retired and then began short-term missionary tours and a writing career. She even rafted the Snake River while playing a harmonica. The interpretation of this milestone is the critical factor in determining its impact.

The change in pace of life also influences the severity of the crisis. Certainly part of this crisis can be attributed to the fact that so many move from the fast lane in life to life on a gravel road within a period of a few weeks. It seems most beneficial for a person to plan a gradual slowing-down period followed by a meaningful retirement. In societies where the elderly are revered and active, the adjustment to retirement may be easier. In our society the severity of the crisis can be seen by the high percentage of those who die before finishing their first retirement year.

Another issue of stress in retirement is financial. Retirement usually brings a marked decline in income. Even when there is sufficient income, one always wonders *if* and *when* it will become eroded away by inflation. The current discussions of the insecurity of social security may increase the stress.

Discussion—Aging

When we discuss aging in today's society, it may be best to think in terms of the "young old" and the "old old." Many people past sixty-five are still vital and active. Our image of a grandmother has changed markedly over the past generation. Although many of the perceived negative aspects of aging are simply myths, there are some real readjustments.

Many have referred to the aging years as the golden years. The golden age beyond sixty-five years is based on the idea that men and women can retire from the work world. While the general public thinks sufficient income for the elderly is a problem, only 15 percent of people over sixty-five report this is a problem. Some people continue to work part-time and many reduce their standard of living. For some there is a crisis when the person who has been independent suddenly becomes dependent emotionally, physically, or economically.

In time, many retired persons just can't do what they once could. Someone else may have to do the gardening, house repairs, mending, and even driving. Often the person's mind is every bit as sharp as it used to be, but the body can't do what the mind tells it to do.[14]

The crisis of old age for the "old old" is really a collection of many crises. For some, the situations just mentioned grow in seriousness, often without any hope of resolution. The loss of sight, hearing, and mobility are generally not physically restored. One's only hope lies in his or her acceptance of limitations.[15]

Many older people are in physical pain. Old injuries come back to haunt them; new injuries cause discomfort. Pain comes and goes or just comes and stays. For a few the quality of life is reduced by pain and/or the anticipation of pain.

For some, loneliness adds to the crisis of aging. Although one study indicated 60 percent of the general population thought the elderly were lonely, only 12 percent of the elderly listed this as a problem.[16] Nevertheless, as children leave, a spouse passes away, friends move or die, and as limitations reduce the sphere of contacts with friends and relatives, loneliness becomes an issue. People who retire soon find just how important the social network of employment was for them. They had a regular routine in their work life, eating lunch or drinking coffee with coworkers with whom they shared their lives. Research indicates that recently widowed spouses have a significantly higher than normal rate of death. Most people maintain their identities in a social context. As other people react to them, they see how they are perceived and therefore who they are. Because of this, interpersonal contacts are a major deterrent to old age crisis.[17]

It's also important for an older person to keep creating, doing, seeing, listening, speaking, and sharing. In short, he or she should get outside of self and get into living. We all need a purpose for living. No one is ever too old to have good reasons to live.[18] One way to add meaning to life is to have goals and attempt to achieve them, and this is particularly true for an older person.[19]

There are many stories of people who have become recognized after they turned sixty-five. Colonel Harland Sanders and Grandma Moses are just two notable examples. President Reagan was elected after age sixty-five and overcame the severe wounds of an assassination attempt. Life can be lived successfully at any age, and the aging person needs to keep this challenge before him- or herself at all times.

Proper intervention can help the elderly client to cope with necessary losses, prevent those that are avoidable, and achieve mutual support systems to combat loneliness.[20]

Common Feelings and Issues for Counselors to Address

Retirement:

- loss of identity associated with career
- loss of peer group
- adjustment of husband and wife being together more
- change in schedule
- feelings about being unproductive or worthless
- lack of schedule and structure
- financial worry

Aging:

- becoming dependent
- adjustment to physical limitations
- loneliness
- adjustment to possibility of living alone
- mental limitations
- loss of possessions and surroundings

CHAPTER SIX

FINANCIAL CRISES

A WHOLE SET OF CRISES has to do with the loss of property. This has a variety of impacts on people, depending upon what the property means to them. The meaning of property varies as well as the degree of personal identity attached to that property. As Christians we are encouraged not to become preoccupied with material goods but to keep our eyes on spiritual matters. Matthew 6:19 even says that if we try to accumulate things we may well suffer some property loss. In spite of all this, Christians do sometimes have crises over the loss of property. They may not suffer as much as unbelievers or the crises may not last as long, but they are, nevertheless, real crises.

Many crises are generated from stressful situations generated by financial or financially related events. In this chapter we would like to consider aspects such as job loss, financial loss, being the victim of a crime, and natural disasters.

UNEMPLOYMENT

Case Example

Bill wants to find work again, but he has little energy and is usually tired. Every day seems to drag on longer than the day before. His shoulders hunch forward, and his face shows the lines of depression. He seems like a hollow robot as he goes from company to company seeking employment. His confidence is gone. He tries not to worry, but the nights are also long and restless. He usually sleeps off and on, intermittently waking up thinking about how his world has changed.

Bill had been with a small manufacturing plant for twelve years. He was settled into the company and had been a responsible employee. Then one afternoon the whole plant was called into a meeting that he'll never forget. They were all told how the changes in the economy had been affecting the company. The president was very sorry, but they had decided to close down and sell the buildings and land to another firm. Bill, along with all the others, sat in disbelief. He was numb when he arrived home and told Shirley. She tried to assure him that everything was fine and that he was still a capable provider for the family. They would get along until he found something else and that would be soon. The words of reassurance bounced off him like arrows hitting armor. They did not console him, nor did they reassure him. The future looked bleak and empty. He could not envision where he would be working, with whom, nor what the boss would be like. Hundreds of questions began racing through his mind. The biggest was where to begin the next day.

Discussion—The Emotional Impact

The crisis of job loss raises many issues for people in light of their identity, sense of security, and feelings of failure. The impact of the loss, of course, varies a great deal depending on factors such as the age of the person, his or her training and educational level, and the type of work in which he or she is employed. There are other factors: Is he or she the sole support of the family? What are the financial reserves? Are friends and relatives available to help? Did the termination come as a surprise?

Often in the case of a skilled laborer, the older the person, the greater the crisis. Yet another observation holds more weight than this one. The extent of the crisis depends on the developmental life-cycle task the person is contemplating. For example, a man in his mid-forties who is already re-evaluating his life and in some ways questioning his self-worth may be much more influenced than a man in his fifties who is secure in his self-identity and is less dependent on his employment for meaning.

Usually the better educated a person is and the more training he or she has in a variety of skills, the more he or she perceives him- or herself to be employable. Depending on the state of the economy, the white collar worker is often in a better position to find new employment than a blue collar worker; a professional often has more influential contacts when it comes to employment. The tradesman or skilled blue collar worker is generally in a better position than the unskilled blue collar worker.

If the spouse is employed, the family may be less injured than if the sole bread winner is terminated. The one remaining income may ease the pressure on house payments and basic necessities.

Some people who live from paycheck to paycheck feel pressure to gain employment rapidly. They may take any job, even if it is unrewarding and less than desirable, to avoid the stress of no income. Where extended families or support networks step in to offer assistance, the crisis stress is markedly decreased.

A recent television news report featured a story on an executive who had just told the employees that the factory was closing. Some long-term employees were asked what they would do next, and many of them said, "I guess I'll go home and think about it." Few people were able to look forward beyond the present moment. Most were headed for the security of their homes in an effort to deal with their initial shock.

When people know a layoff or termination is forthcoming,

they begin preparing in advance, and this minimizes the shock. If a whole section of a plant closes down, those involved have each other for support. The man or woman who loses his or her job because of a performance, personality, or political problem has the additional stress of coping with feelings of failure.

The loss injures the whole family, but it has an initial impact on the person who has lost the job. Have you ever met strangers and noted how they identified themselves to you? Most people, at best, partially describe who they are in terms of their employment. For some, when the job goes, so does the identity. One unemployed man reported a conversation he overheard between his son and a playmate. The two boys were trying to outdo each other, and the playmate declared that his daddy was a carpenter and strong. The man's son then said, "My daddy's a nothing, but he's stronger." The son had hit the father's deepest feelings right on the head. Some men, who relate to the world physically and feel good about being the strongest man in the assembly section or the fastest carpetlayer in the store, sense a loss of masculinity that contributes to the crisis. They may have been proud of and received recognition for their ability, but now the potential for recognition is gone.

Certainly inadequacy becomes a part of the issue. Have I failed? Am I capable? What's wrong with me? I can't do anything right. It is not unusual to see one aspect of life such as unemployment get generalized to the whole personality. Pretty soon the person, in lieu of questioning his or her ability as an engineer, has lowered his or her entire self-worth.

The unemployed may need help to see the value in what they have learned from the previous job. Some people feel they have wasted five prime years because they had only one goal: the next promotion. This needs to be put into perspective. What did they learn at that job that will help them at their next one?

The stress of being an unemployed breadwinner carries social implications as well. What will my friends think? Will people lose respect for me? This sense of embarrassment may color all of a person's relationships.

People report turbulent feelings in their relationships at home. Often husbands will cling close to their wives and then suddenly push away. Life is like the ocean waves—an ongoing vacillation between closeness and distance. In one sense families are unemployed if one of their members is laid off. Families feel the impact and need to be prepared for the inevitable strained relationships. Family members are usually so closely related that they all carry the stress. Depending on the dynamics of the family system, sometimes a child will unconsciously become the stress bearer, the pressure being evident in his or her behavior.

If the job hunting proves to elicit only a long and painful series of "Don't call us, we'll be in touch" replies, the seeker may well lose part of his or her drive and determination. One wife was frustrated because her husband did not get out and look for employment. It was obvious that he was dealing with the pain of being refused and had become discouraged. It is important that family and friends realize the need for support—emotional support. Any offers of financial support need to be considered carefully as they might generate a further loss of self-respect. Instead of outright donations it may be better to suggest loans that have indefinite pay-back dates or short-term work, such as house painting or repairing.

The days become long. The resumés are out. He or she waits for the phone to ring. When it does ring anticipation is frustrated because it's Junior's friend calling to see if he can come over. The highlight of the day is awaiting the mail carrier, and that becomes the reference point for time. Was that good television show on before or after the mail came?

The impact of the unemployment crisis is demonstrated in the higher rates of illness and death associated with job loss. We have observed that even family members of the unemployed have higher rates of destructive behavior, physical illness, and depression than other families not facing the same difficulties.

Common Feelings and Issues for Counselors to Address

- shock to one's sense of security
- fear of financial ruin
- insecurity about basic life needs
- self-condemnation or inadequacy

- self-blame
- possible loss of identity
- fear of loss of respect of others
- strained relationships in the family

Discussion—Financial Assistance and Community Resources

What can be done to help the person facing this crisis? Because he or she may well be feeling somewhat useless, any job around the home or church that has some degree of significance can be very helpful. It is important that he or she be involved and contributing to others, not isolated. Acceptance, recreation, and activity are also important. An unemployed person may need someone outside the family to help him or her evaluate or assess the skills he or she has and therefore the types of employment that might be open.

Many unemployed people develop a routine and make a job out of searching for a position. This eases the crisis as it provides activity, organization, and daily goals. The primary goal of the unemployed person is to find work. The following list of helpful positive activities has been gleaned from people we have counseled. You might want to share these with clients who are out of work.

1. Make a list of job skills and/or jobs you think you can perform.
2. Make a list of potential employers.
3. Develop a resumé—ask others for input.
4. Mail resumé and a cover letter to your list of potential employers.
5. Mail resumé to employment agencies.
6. Personally contact all your potential employers. Sell them on what you can do for them.
7. Tell potential employers why you want to work for their company (i.e., they have a good reputation).
8. Follow up all interviews with a letter or a phone call.
9. If an employer clearly cannot hire you, ask for referrals to similar employers who may be hiring. Follow up with a thank-you letter for the referrals.
10. If your job skills are not marketable in your area, con-

sider attending a trade school to learn new skills that are in high demand in your area.

11. Consider using part-time or temporary employment to get a full-time position or training.

When people are out of work they need to know that others believe in them. This becomes critical when they are turned down by prospective employers and feel the whole world is against them. Eventually they will find employment and the crisis will subside. But you need to be prepared to assist for several months if necessary. Their adjustment is not complete until they are settled into a new position, and even then they may carry job performance anxiety for months or years. While in the past men have been most impacted by the loss of a job, women are now experiencing many of the same feelings.

In the case of involuntary unemployment, all states, in conjunction with the unemployment insurance program of the federal government, provide at least twenty-six weeks of benefits. This basic amount of protection may vary from about $105 to $278 per week in maximum benefits.[1] All unemployed persons, no matter what the circumstances of their unemployment, should contact their local state unemployment office. At worst, they will find they aren't eligible for benefits. At best, they will be compensated.

Additionally, from time to time, normally in association with an economic down-turn, unemployment benefits have been extended over a longer period of time. When unemployment insurance benefits have been exhausted, the unemployed should ask about the possibility of an extension.

The vast majority of people don't like to ask for handouts, but there are times when we all need help of one kind or another. It is not immoral or wrong to apply for social welfare. To the contrary, persons who are faced with a financial crisis because of unemployment should make use of resources for which they've paid taxes. To a large degree, the government has taken over from the church and many other community groups the function of helping the financially distressed. When welfare does not meet the basic minimum standards of need, the church and other community agencies should be contacted for supplemental help.

FINANCIAL LOSS

Discussion

Whenever the concept of financial crisis is presented, many people immediately imagine the conditions of the early 1930s when hard times were widespread. When the stock market crashed, successful businessmen jumped out of office windows to their deaths. The emotional pain that accompanied their financial loss was too much for them. This stereotype may not apply at all to many situations of financial loss.

The crisis of financial loss can be produced from a variety of events. A business investment that looked as if it would return a sure profit goes sour and all one's investment is lost. The economy turns downward and a person who has a lot of debt loses his or her assets. A family is secure in the fact that the house is burglar proof, until one evening when they return late to find the silverware, television, and stereo gone. An earthquake or tornado destroys a family's one big asset—their house, which isn't covered by insurance. Medical bills constantly drain a person's bank account, as a congenital heart problem renders her uninsurable.

Most Christians don't want to attach undue significance and meaning to money or materialism, yet most of us are very involved in what we have acquired. We have zero material assets when we arrive in the world and we take zero assets with us when we die, yet between those two dates we attach a great deal of meaning to our possessions.

The impact of financial crisis depends heavily on a person's interpretation of the value of financial resources. How much meaning do they have for the person? How closely linked are they to one's identity? Many people have been influenced by our materialistic society so that their self-worth is tied to their financial status. If they have a bigger house, bigger income, bigger car, they feel more valuable as people. Their lives revolve around acquisition of possessions. For them a financial loss crisis becomes extremely difficult and painful.

Other factors include the amount of a loss as compared to assets and income. If a millionaire loses twenty thousand dollars, he made a bad deal. If a family with a modest income loses twenty thousand dollars, they may also lose their dream of owning a home. When you know of someone going through a financial crisis it is useful to be aware of his or her ability to recoup the loss, as this will surely influence the impact of the loss. Just how will this change his or her life? What does this person value that this loss will shift? How will this loss change him or her or what will he or she learn or experience? Five years from now, how will he or she be different than he or she would be if this hadn't happened?

When counseling people in this crisis, we think it is useful to focus on the future. When things look so dark there is great need for hope, which can carry people through times of great despair. When there is despair and no hope, life becomes intolerable. Perhaps you know of others who have gone through similar times and have recouped. Their stories might relay hope. For example, one couple invested their life savings in a land development project in California. The profits promised to be high and they were assured that they'd be set for life. Just as they thought all was going well, environmental concerns caused delay after delay until they lost almost all of their investment. Where did they land? They are now in midlife. They live in a pleasant, modest home. Both are working at jobs they seem to enjoy. They are friendly, enthusiastic people who thoroughly enjoy life. They have lost much, but in some ways they have also gained much. They lost their nest egg, but life didn't end.

Some people believe that their financial loss means that they will soon be sitting on a couch with holes in it. They further deduce that nobody will want to come to their house. Because they cannot provide enough, they fear that others will withdraw. Reassurance by word and deed can be very supportive. One needs to be sensitive to social considerations. You don't plan a Dutch-treat evening out with them at an expensive restaurant. And to pay their way to everything may only cause more self-recrimination.

If theirs was a financial loss that was caused or compounded by personality traits such as impulsiveness or poor planning, you might want to think preventatively. They may need you to help them understand that they overcommit or have an unrealistic view of life. Perhaps they need education or knowledge about financial principles. They may want to attend classes or seminars or get books that can be useful in financial management.

Some people in financial crisis have gotten there because they have listened to poor advice. Many people who claim to be knowledgeable about money simply are unethical swindlers. People feel doubly hurt when they lose their money this way.

People in financial crises are particularly vulnerable to get-rich-quick schemes and should be advised to watch out for disreputable signs of anyone offering a great business deal or selling any financial service.[2] Needing a quick decision, a very high or rapid rate of return, or a guaranteed safety of investment are all warning signs that this may not be a good investment. We've known of situations where persons of questionable ability or ethics have come into a church and hurt a number of people financially. Sometimes the victims were doubly victimized because they were already in financial trouble when they made these bad investments. Reputations should always be checked.

You may refer someone in financial crisis to an expert who can provide financial advice. Some people may be viewing their financial situation as impossible, whereas an expert may notice alternatives that have not been considered. One couple was sure they were losing their house because their income had dropped drastically when the man's commissions were cut. But a financial advisor helped them reorganize some payments so they were able to keep their home. What a tremendous relief from the burden of loss! With that part of the financial crisis behind them, they were free to deal with their long-term plans.

Sometimes this crisis may also mean that friends dig into their own pockets to help directly. We don't like to think of this, but Christians are called to be generous with their own money. In the midst of their own poverty the early church gave generously to their fellow Christians (2 Cor. 8). Yet this must be done in such a way as not to destroy the person in the process. He or she may lose self-worth, be self-condemning, feel obligated, or become dependent as a result of such financial assistance.

Several men from one church were experiencing financial difficulties and being hard pressed to support their families. In lieu of giving them money, another church member hired them to put an addition on his home. They felt good about the work. He enhanced the value of his property while providing them a way of obtaining income to alleviate their financial crisis.

You might suggest these key steps to work out of financial crisis:

1. Gather all current financial records and set up a checklist of all obligations.[3]

2. Prepare a budget based on current and new future conditions. This will serve as both a planning and control tool.[4]

3. Contact creditors if your budget income can't meet budget expenses. Work out with them a realistic payment schedule. If the person in financial trouble attempts to work with lenders they often make similar attempts to cooperate. It's when a person does nothing that problems begin.

4. Make a list of assets that can be sold to cover urgent financial needs. Sell as needed. (Don't overlook simple things, such as newspapers in the garage, used tools, etc. A garage sale can provide groceries for a week or more.)

5. Make a list of all the extra jobs you can undertake. Again, simple part-time odds-and-ends jobs can get you out of crisis.

6. Contact people who owe you money and see if they can repay you soon so as to meet your crisis need.

7. In extreme financial crisis, church members can sometimes get help from a church fund set aside for those in need.

8. Financial emergencies can sometimes be handled with loans from credit unions, banks, or family members. You will need some collateral (you may have more than you think you do) and the ability to repay.

9. If the above cannot be done in total or in part, it is wise to meet with a certified financial planner, certified public accountant, or other qualified financial advisor for help. Should your financial professional be a salesperson for financial products he or she may not charge directly for the services, but his or her advice could very well be biased. We feel that it is best to pay a professional who is not a salesperson at the outset.

Common Feelings and Issues for Counselors to Address

- loss of identity and self-worth
- panic
- despair
- self-condemnation for poor investment choices
- over-reactive distrust
- needed financial advice

Crime Victim

Case Example

She comes home from work and does not notice the open door until she reaches the sidewalk. Perhaps her son has left it open. That wouldn't be unusual. She enters the living room and sees that someone has broken in. She knows not to touch anything and calls the police. The detective comes and routinely reviews with her in a businesslike fashion what she saw and what is missing. She thinks the detective is impersonal, but later realizes that if she spent day after day filling out burglary reports she probably would be impersonal too. She is a Christian and is not caught up in possessions as the meaning of her life. Yet the loss of the jewelry her mother had given her hits her hard. It's not the value of the jewelry; it's the irreplaceable memories and meanings that she mourns. She questions why God would allow this to happen to her.

Discussion

Victims of crime are naturally humiliated, shocked, and angry. They realize they are singled out and taken advantage of and helpless. The anger that goes with being victimized is often as related to the injustice of it all as it is to the loss itself.

I recall stepping out of the house one bright sunny Sunday morning only to find that someone had stolen two evergreen trees right out of our yard. Was I ever angry! I had done nothing to precipitate such an act. Someone had simply "ripped us off." No doubt part of my anger was my sense of loss of control over my own property. I was helpless to prevent or stop the crime. The situation is even worse when people enter your home and rob you. How dare someone come into *your* living room, *your* kitchen, *your* bedroom? Since a home is a place of safety and privacy, your very sense of security is shaken to the core.

Recently a man had his television, cameras, and stereo stolen during the afternoon while he was at work. A day or so later he was still in a state of shock. He was bitter. Since the thief had apparently entered by a window, the victim had gone out that evening, purchased a big bag of spikes, and nailed shut every window in the house. His sense of security was lost. He was discouraged and depressed. In the midst of his crisis he needed support.

The "who done it?" question raises issues of personality, mistrust, and prejudice. In speculating about what happened, this man blamed some of his friends or the racial minority family in the neighborhood. (It is true that neighborhood conditions have a relationship to crime rates.)[5] Then neighborhood speculation ran wild. Prejudices and fears were expressed as others contemplated ways to defend themselves. Perhaps people feel more secure when they think they know from whom they are protecting themselves.

People can be victims of crime perpetrated by their own families. *Harassment, aggravated assault,* and *reckless endangerment* are terms frequently used to describe spousal abuse.[6] A complex series of financial crises are associated with these kinds of crimes. Many of the financial problems can be associated with divorce and separation. In addition, legal costs, medical expenses, and therapy costs can result in a financial crisis that compounds the already existent interpersonal crisis. Professional legal, psychological, and financial help will often be needed in this type of compound crisis.

Common Feelings and Issues for Counselors to Address

- humiliation
- helplessness
- breach of sense of security
- anger
- realization that one was "picked out of the crowd" as a victim

- loss of irreplaceable heirlooms; loss of family history
- lack of control of life
- issues of mistrust and prejudice

Natural Disasters

Case Example

I lived in southern California in 1971 when an earthquake of considerable magnitude shook the area. Most families, like my own, suffered the loss of some broken glasses that bounced out of cupboards, but others lost their homes and some lost loved ones. Even those who suffered limited physical damage or loss experienced an emotional crisis. Many mental health clinics set up groups in which people could talk about the earthquake. Some people became extremely tense and anxious; others could not sleep. They suddenly were confronted with the reality that their lives were not under their control. The home they valued as a sanctuary of security was a threat when the walls suddenly collapsed. The secure ground they walked on suddenly shook their feet out from under them. In some homes half the garage floor ended up six inches higher than the other half. Now that is a visible reminder that the "secure" earth isn't secure. Security in oneself, one's ability to control life, and one's safety dissolved.

At other places and times the disaster is a tornado, hurricane, volcano, fire, or flood. And now there are social crises that could have similar effects: terrorist acts, discovery of chemical waste deposits, such as Love Canal, or nuclear malfunction, such as Three Mile Island.[7] Whatever the precipitating event, the issues are similar.

Discussion

The personal issues faced by individuals affected by disaster are varied, depending on the extent of their loss. If, for example, a tornado destroys some houses in one block and not others, people try to figure out why. Questions abound: Was our home destroyed because we are being punished? Was our house left standing because we were good? Should we feel guilty if our neighbor's houses were destroyed and ours was not? Do we take this as a sign that God favors us and blesses us because we are good or does he love us more? Many people begin to think of God as a powerful parental figure and attribute all kinds of motives to him.

The intense anxiety is followed by shock and disbelief. This is followed by relief that the disaster itself has passed. Imagine the intensity of the fear that would come from knowing you nearly lost your life. Of course you survived but you immediately start wondering about others who are not with you. For example, my sister was at a church service in northern Indiana in the spring of 1965 when one of the ushers interrupted the message and asked everyone to lie down on the floor because a tornado was headed directly for the church. There must have been a few minutes of intense prayer! Although the tornado destroyed many houses on two sides of the church, it did not hit the sanctuary. What relief when the noisy winds moved off into the distance. The people in the church were spared, but immediately they asked questions about friends and relatives who couldn't be reached because phone lines were down and trees blocked the roads. For some, these experiences are immobilizing.

A community that is hit by a natural disaster rallies together and gives mutual support. This, of course, is a major factor in the adjustment process. People help each other in surprising and heartwarming ways. They pull together to raise each other out of "the pit." However, things aren't quite the same when a person goes through a disaster, such as a house fire, alone. Such a person or family receives help, but obviously their need is more solitary and lacks a camaraderie that comes from knowing others are going through a similar situation. In either type of situation, it is important for victims to talk through the crisis[8] so they feel they are not alone.

A natural disaster crisis is so large in the life of a family that it usually becomes a milestone or a reference point: Remember the vacation we took a couple years after "the fire"? It becomes a point from which events of lesser significance are placed in sequence.

When people's lives have been threatened, their property loss is initially minimized. The first reaction is "We lost part of our home, but everyone in the family will be all right." The actual loss of property and finances becomes an issue only later, when they are overwhelmed with mixed feelings. Economic loss can compound and extend the terrible consequences of natural disaster, which is ultimately so psychologically devastating because it and its long-term effects are so uncontrollable.

God becomes a key part of the natural disaster crisis. Researchers have found that people who suffer loss usually express or are aware of aggressive feelings toward the source of their loss.[9] As a Christian counselor, it is important for you to deal with a victim's anger toward God, the "Source" of natural disaster. It is quite useless to ignore anger toward God or encourage its denial. Initially, it is best not to cite all the reasons why it is illogical to be angry at God. Just listen. Some need to be reminded that God is big enough to handle their anger. Since God is all-knowing, no one can hide feelings and thoughts from him (Pss. 33:13–15; 139:2; Acts 15:8). People have a hard time reconciling until they can identify and articulate their hurt. The best way to reframe anger is to point out that it arises from an underlying feeling or hurt. Once the person identifies the hurt, he or she can pray about the feeling. You need to let the person talk through his or her hurt with God. This may be hard for some who have felt chastised or rejected by a powerful father figure, yet you can help them as they make their decisions about what to do with their hurt. Ideally, they will develop a sense of acceptance of reality and grow into reconciliation with God.

Eventually people begin to get their lives back in order and back into a routine. The restructuring that comes from slowly reorganizing has a very therapeutic effect. Part of the anxiety can be dissipated by the manual labor (somewhat like occupational therapy) but also from knowing friends are helping them get life back to normal. The move to action gives the victim the sense of coping, even conquering, rather than being a passive victim.

Giving physical help to someone who is facing this crisis is one of the best possible healing experiences. Maybe you help shovel the mud out of the living room or tear down the splintered beams or help pick up debris from fields so crops can be cultivated. This kind of help focuses on the future and the rebuilding of lives.

Common Feelings and Issues for Counselors to Address

- loss of security of home
- loss of control of environment
- fear of death or injury; fear of recurrence
- loss of economic base; creation of major indebtedness
- guilt if loss is comparatively minor
- anger at God
- worry about fear in children
- confusion or remorse (is God punishing us?)

CHAPTER SEVEN

SPIRITUAL CRISES

EACH OF US HAS BEEN MADE in the image of God (Gen. 1:26, 27). God has a unique relationship with humans who were created with a spiritual component that his other creations lack.[1] While humans need to be seen as whole beings, each aspect of a human should be considered in dealing with any crisis. Every crisis can have a profound impact on the spiritual part of the person. Conversely, spiritual problems can create stress within the individual to the point that a crisis takes place. In this chapter we will explore what we call spiritual crises.

CONVERSION

Case Example

Tears trickle down Linda's face as she quietly expresses her burden, her emptiness. Yes, she wants to accept Jesus Christ as her Savior. Susan, her friend, puts her arm around Linda as they sit together. Linda asks Jesus to forgive her sins. Both young women hold each other and Linda feels Susan's concern. Susan nearly explodes with joy, knowing she has been a real help to Linda and has played a key role in winning her to the Lord.

Not all conversion experiences are so dramatic, but Linda is on "cloud nine" when she goes back to her apartment. She feels like a new person. Never has she felt so at peace within herself.

In the morning, Linda still feels great. She is so excited she calls her mother to tell her about her new-found joy.

Linda can't remember her parents attending church other than for a few weddings. They just never talked much about God or church. As the phone rings at her mother's apartment, Linda wonders how she should phrase her announcement. When Mother answers, Linda says excitedly, "Hi, Mom." After a little chitchat, Linda continues, "I accepted Jesus Christ as my Savior and Lord last night." There is a long, awkward pause. Linda tries to explain, "Last night I went to a church near here and heard an evangelist. What he said showed me clearly that all the burdens I've been carrying around could be taken off me by Jesus Christ."

There is another pause, then Linda's mother says, "Linda, I'm glad you're so happy." As her mother unenthusiastically says that whatever makes Linda happy will make her happy, Linda begins to feel that her mother doesn't really understand. Mother has to get to work so the phone conversation ends abruptly. Linda feels a little let down and disappointed. She doesn't know what she'd wanted from Mother, but this wasn't it!

That day at college Linda shares with her friend Sherry, who just listens. After hearing Linda's story, Sherry sums up her feelings, "Linda, don't get too carried away with all this religious stuff." Linda did not expect that response and again feels a little let down.

All day long one rebuff after another pushes Linda from joy to frustration and even doubt. Maybe she can't live up to being a good Christian, she thinks. Maybe people see something in her she hadn't seen in herself.

The only thing that makes her day worthwhile is talking to her Christian employer. Ken is really excited for her and promises to pray for her. At least someone understands, someone cares.

Discussion

Linda's experience has happened many times over the years. Most people just don't really understand the excitement of the person who has accepted Jesus Christ.

Most persons who convert from the religion of their family to Christianity are going to face a crisis. Normally, conversion will precipitate a straightforward rejection of the convert's actions if not complete rejection of him or her as a member of the family. The rejection process may be subtle. The converting family member may no longer be invited to certain family gatherings. Some people may not speak; others may indicate rejection with body language; yet others may not drop by as frequently as before. Converts may feel cut off from the past, family, and friends. If they do not get nurturing care from new-found friends in Christ, their personal crises can take on very serious dimensions. They may be suddenly socially isolated. While they will have Jesus Christ with them, they will find it difficult to grow if fellow Christians don't take an interest in them.

For others, the crisis that accompanies conversion may be precipitated by the reaction of one family member who is in some way threatened by another becoming "born again." For example, a husband may feel distress at a wife's conversion because she is now absorbed in religion. He may feel ignored or worry about nonacceptance from their friends. He may resent some of the changes in her values and behavior, putting stress on the marriage. It is easy to blame an "outside force," such as a spouse's faith, for causing marital problems.

We think each person needs to have a relationship with Jesus Christ. Carl M. Sweazy has said, "The supreme need of every man is Jesus Christ."[2] It follows that the person who recognizes this need will want to have it met unless the other aspects of his or her life prevent the whole person from converting.

Although we do not want to deny the work and power of the Holy Spirit, we do note that social influences may have a profound impact on a person who has converted to Christianity. Friends, relatives, and co-workers all play a vital role in one's feeling of self-worth. When the individual's social network is hostile to his or her conversion, it is difficult for the person to go through the crisis without a new social network that will support the decision.

For some, a conversion not only generates a crisis but is in part produced by an existing crisis. Based on a study done a few years ago, 57 percent of the persons in the sample stated that a crisis in their lives was associated with their conversion.[3] Many a person decides to become a Christian in an attempt to overcome a crisis situation. If the individual experiencing conversion is not incorporated into an organized group, there is a great possibility that the individual will slip away.[4] The church needs to see conversion as a process that only begins with an acceptance of Christ as Savior.

What specifically should be done with a person who is in the conversion process, especially when the conversion is prompted by a preexisting crisis?

1. Determine if there was a preexisting crisis in addition to conversion. Use intervention methods suggested in this book to work through the preexisting crisis.
2. Try to find out how the conversion crisis is interrelated to the preexisting crisis.
3. Help the person develop a support network of Christians.
4. Help the person get integrated into a church and a small group in the church.
5. Be sensitive to the development of additional crises, such as rejection of the convert by family or significant others.
6. See that he or she is introduced to Christian teachings and lifestyle. The convert needs to know how to understand and use the Bible.
7. Teach and encourage the convert to develop an effective prayer life.

Common Feelings and Issues for Counselors to Address

- lack of understanding from significant others
- rejection from significant others
- personal joy met with resistance

- emotional and spiritual relief without full understanding of experience
- uncertainty about the future and what to expect
- change in family relationships due to change in life priorities; possible conflict
- loss of close social relationships
- issues of worthiness

Disappointment and Loss in Spiritual Leaders

Discussion

Spiritual crises can arise from disappointment in spiritual leaders and can take place in a variety of settings. Most people never have to face the crisis of disappointment in a spiritual leader, but we want to address the issue so you can be aware and respond well to those who do.

Sooner or later in most churches a pastor leaves and a new one arrives. The arrival of the new leader is usually, but not always, a positive experience for church members. In most churches, the new leader is very acceptable as his or her strengths have been emphasized. However, on occasion in some churches extreme disappointment in a spiritual leader can generate a crisis.

Even in churches where the past has been a relatively pleasant experience, crisis events may be sparked by a too-high level of expectation. The future looks bright when a new pastor comes to a church. People are confident that any minor problems of the past will be resolved; all those things left undone will now be taken care of. Hope and excitement abound during the first six months to two years of a new pastor's tenure. But after the honeymoon is over, the reality that the pastor does not "walk on water" becomes painfully clear.

Some people expect the impossible from pastors. Somehow they are supposed to know what is happening—even though no one communicates with them. They are supposed to be human but only within certain limits. For example, pastors should show no negative feelings. These unrealistic expectations can lead to disappointment within members and often within pastors and their families, too.

Some congregational members tend to project their feelings about former pastors, television or radio preachers, and especially all-sufficient father figures onto the pastor. The picture these members have of the pastor is distorted by their own past experiences and expectations.

Crises come about when a pastor does not do, say, or act as the congregational members desire. The crisis usually leads to some disruption in the relationship between parishioner and pastor. If the disappointed member attempts to resolve the problem by aligning other members to his or her side, the grievance and stress may, in extreme situations, divide the congregation. If some members leave, those who stay in the church go through some grief because their relationship with the departing parties may never be the same. In time, resolution of the grief takes place to the degree that people forgive—although the conflict is not forgotten. If a similar incident later begins to develop, the individual may respond as he or she learned to do in the previous experience.

Frequently pastors unwittingly stir up church members' old pain or resentments toward authority figures. Members may feel attacked from the pulpit when no such intention was in the pastor's mind. Anger at a former pastor or spiritual leader or disappointment in one's parents may be projected onto the pastor who unintentionally stirs the old feelings. A very limited issue can be expanded far beyond its original focus when past feelings are resurrected.

When thinking about one's own ministry to others, it is often easy to forget about church leaders. Most people think of them as ministering to others and forget that they need encouragement, especially at times of crisis in their lives. One minister recently said that he gets criticism, but he seldom, if ever, gets compliments or expressions of appreciation. His life is one of encouragement deprivation.

When counseling with those who have been disappointed by the behavior of religious leaders, it is appropriate to help them focus on their expectations of church leaders. Help your clients recognize that all leaders are human and have areas of weakness. We all wish this weren't so, but it is unreasonable to anticipate perfection. Those hurting from this crisis need support as they struggle through their disappointment. Their disappointment with others shouldn't disrupt their own continued spiritual growth and development nor should they use their anger in ways that disrupt others' spiritual growth. They need encouragement to channel their emotions toward growth and understanding rather than destruction.

Crises may also be generated for congregational members when, one Sunday morning at the conclusion of the sermon, the pastor resigns. The aisles and narthex of the church buzz with conversations about the pastor's leaving. Underneath the communication is a layer of emotion generated by the loss of an authority figure. Some may feel hurt, some abandoned, some insulted (aren't we good enough?), some angry from rejection; others may feel relief or even joy.

When one pastor resigned (effective in a few months), one of the long-term church staff members took the news so personally that she refused to speak to him for the rest of his tenure. This otherwise mature and capable woman spun into such a crisis that she lost her usual life-coping skills. She became extremely bitter and welled up with anger. Other members of the church reacted, but more like lost sheep without a shepherd. They had to be reminded that the pastor was leaving, not God himself. Depending on the height of the pedestal on which the pastor has been placed, the level of crisis may reach significant proportions. To soften the blow, a pastor might reassure the congregation of personal, continued concern for their well-being and give names, addresses, and phone numbers of people who could help the church during the time they are without a pastor. (Denominational organizations help here.)

Common Feelings and Issues for Counselors to Address

- betrayal of trust
- anger and resentment
- general mistrust of authority figures
- crushed, hurt, abandoned
- resurrection and transference of old anger or disappointment

- seeking agreement and reassurance from peers
- unrealistic expectations

Conflicting Views of Truth

Case Example

Irene is really excited about being part of a newly formed Bible study in her church. She's a new Christian and wants to learn. Her need for Christian fellowship is of particular importance because her husband, John, is not a believer. In fact, he thinks she is silly, being so religious.

Jane takes her to the first Bible study, which is held at Laura's home. Laura begins the meeting with prayer which includes a petition that the Holy Spirit guide her and illuminate each person present. Irene is impressed with the beginning, although she feels like a spiritual lightweight. During the course of the study, Laura made a point of saying how terrible it is that the teenage girls in the church are allowed to wear lipstick. Irene is a bit surprised by this comment; she'd never heard that women shouldn't wear lipstick.

On their way home, Irene and Jane talk about the Bible study. During the course of the discussion Irene brings up the issue of lipstick. Jane smiles, "You need to understand that Laura has a real thing about lipstick because she is afraid of what kind of girls her five boys will marry." Irene is a bit more confused. She wants to know if there is some sort of church or biblical rule on the subject. Jane says she doesn't know of one but she thinks Laura feels there is something in the Bible about wearing make-up.

Irene doesn't know what to make of all this. Yet in her attempt to do what is "right," she starts to check with other women in the church. An issue that many wish would remain submerged is again floating around because of Irene's wanting to do "right."

During the next six months a major battle shapes up in the church. There are three camps: One thinks Laura is right. A second claims that Laura is going to drive the teenagers away from the church over a nonexistent rule. But the majority of the church is in the third camp, the grandstand sitters. For some, the entire thing is funny; for others, it is a tragic fight. As time passes, each side finds Bible verses to back their positions. Some women in the church begin to avoid each other. About five months into the battle, people are being pushed to join one group or the other. Finally, Laura has had enough. She is sure the pastor is against her, too, so she and her family finally leave the church. In time the church returns to "normal," minus Laura, her family, and many of her friends.

Discussion

"What is the truth?" People have always struggled with this question. In knowing Jesus Christ we know the truth, for Jesus Christ is the Way, the Truth, and the Life (John 14:6). Yet over the centuries, Christians have debated some areas of truth. Do you have to be baptized in order to be saved? Must you have a dispensational view in order to be a "real" Christian? Is the *King James Version* the only really authentic translation of the Bible? These and many hundreds of questions have served to create crises in the lives of many Christians. People have left individual churches, or even the church, over such questions. We cannot even attempt to deal with the questions themselves. Rather, we will deal with the crises often created in the lives of believers over theological issues.

Christians face a major problem of determining which are the critical issues. Which issues are central to our faith and which issues are merely a matter of personal interpretation or opinion? If Christians could agree on a clear definition of what is essential and what is not, many of the serious conflicts that exist in the church would not exist.

Two people who do not agree theologically still can talk to each other and show Christian love. Some Christians who are bitter and mean toward fellow Christians with whom they disagree are a poor example for the world. Christ told us to love even our enemies; certainly we should be able to love Christians with whom we disagree.

The type of battle described in the case example happens in churches with great regularity and generates a series of crises. Finding the truth becomes more than a momentary problem. It is a continual point of stress within the church and may leave long-term scars. There is a strong tension between avoiding false teachings, which are rampant today, and getting off on issues that are not foundational to the truth. The crisis that develops can spread and involve extended families, Christians and non-Christians alike.

There are several thoughts to keep in mind when dealing with the crisis of conflicts over the truth.

1. Often people become personally invested in their view of the truth; to challenge their view of the truth is to challenge them as persons.
2. Bystanders get angry because they are pressured into choosing sides. They are expected to make choices that they see as only hurting them.
3. Some people do choose sides more to feel a part of a group rather than because they really believe the "truth."
4. The real issue often gets lost in the struggle for power, position, and prestige.
5. There are usually casualties in these crises. The question might be asked, "Was the price worth the gain?"
6. There will be an extended time for healing within the church after the crisis has passed. The scars may last as long as the church does.
7. While confrontation is biblical, there are Christlike ways to confront which can help the church rather than hurt it.

The way most churches confront false teachings has resulted in much pain, yet there are times that such a confronting crisis cannot be avoided if a church is to be based on truth. There are many crises that have ended badly. To avoid this, the principles of dealing with crisis at the end of the book should be applied to the church as though it were a living organism going through a crisis.

Common Feelings and Issues for Counselors to Address

- competitive desire to win argument; power struggle
- self-righteousness
- feeling unappreciated and rejected
- feeling of not fitting in
- withdrawal

- victim of discrimination or injustice
- lust
- self-pity
- resentment
- justification of position; need to prove self correct
- hurt; anger for personal attack
- desire to pull others into conflict to gain support
- paranoia

Church Separation and Rejection

Case Example

For five years Ed has taught the fifth grade at the Elm Avenue Church. The boys and girls all love him. He cares for each of them and everyone knows it. Ed is now thirty-five and has never married. At a deacon's meeting, Mr. Sand questions the wisdom of a thirty-five-year-old bachelor teaching a class. He feels only married men should teach Sunday school children. The majority of the board knows that Ed is doing a good job and his single status doesn't bother them. He has dated several fine Christian women over the years, but he hasn't yet found the Lord's gift to him. The board doesn't go along with Mr. Sand, but one Sunday morning Ed overhears Mr. Sand talking to another man in the church. Mr. Sand implies that there must be something wrong with a man who's thirty-five and not married. Ed is shattered. He doesn't say a word. All afternoon he ponders what he's heard. That night he goes to the pastor who prays with Ed after reassuring him of support.

Apparently Mr. Sand is not happy about losing in the board meeting and he rallies several families around him. One family has a boy in Ed's class. Several months before, Ed had sent this boy out of the class for misbehaving and his parents were embarrassed. Needless to say they are willing to help get rid of this man.

Ed is becoming uncomfortable. Finally, after much prayer he feels it is best for him to give up the class. The students are disappointed, angry, and hurt at losing their favorite teacher. The pastor of the church is very conciliatory toward Ed, who sees anything less than reinstatement as a vote of no confidence. Ed decides to look for a new church.

As a result of this battle two boys drop out of Sunday school. Neither of the children's parents attended the church, and so contact with those two families is lost. Both boys experience a crisis in the loss of their friend Ed. They deal with their crisis by getting away from the site of the pain, the church.

Discussion

We have all been aware of people joining our churches; but we tend to be less aware of the people who leave and the crises they go through. People leave churches for many reasons including: moving from the community, marriage to someone from a different church, rejection of parental values, changes of religious views or affiliation, internal dissension in the church, feelings of being rejected or ignored by the church, change in key people in the church, and being asked to leave the church.

The longer and greater the involvement in the church, the more intense and extended will be the adjustment for the individual leaving the church. Most people who leave churches, in fact, go through a crisis of grief and loss.

Many families drop out of the church as a result of moves. The crisis of leaving the old church can result in family or individuals just dropping church attendance from their schedules. This appears to happen most frequently when the person dropping out has attended church because of family pressures or some vague sense of duty.

Some people who go from a small church, where they have been very active, to a very large church get lost in the crowd and in time drop out of the church altogether. On the other hand, some people who suffer from church burnout will seek a larger church in which to hide. A geographic move is one way to deal with church-member burnout.

Many people handle relational conflicts by leaving the church or by making some contact with another church. When they do so, they are often prompted by intense feelings of rejection or betrayal.

Indifference or nonacceptance within a church may produce

painful feelings of rejection that prompt a church member to drop out. This is especially common for childless single adults beyond age thirty and people who have physical handicaps. The blind, deaf, and paralyzed have particularly difficult experiences because they can't "keep up with" or participate as fully as nonhandicapped persons. With very minor adjustments in program planning and with a little personal patience and sensitivity, these valuable people could feel included in church activities. The mentally retarded or socially different also have a difficult time being accepted by the church. By simple neglect they may be rejected. A person wearing odd clothing, having peculiar speech patterns, or being of a different social, economic, or cultural background can be at risk for the stress of nonacceptance.

There are a number of steps people within churches can take to prevent the crisis people face when they leave because they feel rejected.

1. Accept the fact that all of us are unique and have been created by God.

2. Since everyone has some limitations, a church should be accommodating and aware of others' limitations.

3. Attempt to consider all people the way Christ does without regard to class or social or marital standing.

4. Make a commitment to find ways to reach out in love to others. Attitudes needed to be successful in this Christian responsibility are described in the following Scriptures:

Love your neighbor	Leviticus 19:18
Love God with all your heart	Matthew 22:37
Love even your enemies	Matthew 5:44
Love one another	1 John 3:23
Reconcile as reconciled	2 Corinthians 5:18, 19

Disrupted Spiritual Life—Doubt, Anger at God, Guilt

Case Examples

One day a young man came to his pastor and asked if what his high school teacher said was true: that there is no God. The pastor spent over an hour attempting to prove that God does exist. A troubled, doubting young man went out of the pastor's office; maybe what he had believed all his life was not true.

Teenagers are not the only people who have doubts about the existence of God or the role of Jesus Christ. Many adults who have not received the answer to a prayer become confused and build up a reserve of doubt. Still other people question why God does what he does. Their questioning leads to spiritual doubt. The fact is that many if not all people at some time have doubt about their faith or the very existence of God. When people cannot cope with these doubts they often leave the church or find some way to act out their frustration. For some, the fear and guilt of recognized doubt produces almost a panic reaction. Often people need to question their faith in order to own it. Doubt in itself does not need to produce a crisis.

We believe in Jesus Christ out of faith, or do we? The focal point of the crisis of doubt is when people either attempt to prove God's existence (rather than having faith that he exists) or demand that God does what they want (as if he were having to earn their trust). Faith and trust are not a real part of either scenario. The best way to overcome doubt is to recall that by *faith* a person develops a *relationship* with God and his Son.

The particular young man who spent time with his pastor did not stay away from the church. A decade later he began to realize that spiritual truth is found in faith. Less than two-and-a-half decades later he became a pastor himself, having grown through the crisis of doubt.

Henry loved his mother very much. It is not surprising that he became bitter toward God when his mother died. Why hadn't God spared her life? How could a loving God allow his mother to die in such a painful way? Forty years went by and Henry was still very angry at God. Doubting that God was a loving being, he wanted nothing to do with him or his Son, Jesus Christ. One day another crisis entered into Henry's life; he, too, contracted cancer. For two years he suffered from the same enemy that had taken his mother. But something happened in Henry. He became a Christian. His doubts and anger were converted to a relationship with God and to a spiritual devotion. The one regret he had was that he had missed so many years with his Lord.

Doubting and being angry with God are but two of the causes of disruption of our spiritual lives. Another reason for spiritual disruption is unresolved guilt.

Janis is an attractive woman of forty-one. Her husband is a reasonably successful businessman. Seldom does Jack, her husband, get home before seven at night. There is very little romance in their marriage and communications have become increasingly poor over the past several years. Both Janis and Jack are aware that their bodies are aging. Janis fears that Jack will leave her for another woman, which is the scenario that ended the marriages of several of her friends.

The marriage totters along until one day when Janis meets her girlfriend's brother, visiting from New Jersey. Everytime Janis visits her girlfriend, Fred is there. He is attractive, interesting, and recently divorced. Janis learns that he likes the area so much that he is trying to find a job in the community. The more she learns about Fred, the more she likes him. He communicates well with her, demonstrates real interest in her, and is simply fun to be with. Over a period of a month Fred and Janis become more than good friends, they become lovers. Janis has a guilty conscience, yet her need for attention and affection is so great that she pushes it to the back of her mind.

Janis's guilt is great, especially when she thinks about her children learning of her affair. Eventually Jack finds out and Janis tries to reconcile with him, but that fails. Jack doesn't want a divorce but he doesn't work to improve their relationship. Janis can't live with the gossip that springs up, especially at her church, so she stops attending. One day Janis loads her clothes into the compact car, leaves home, and files for divorce.

Over the next several years guilt turns into bitterness for both Jack and Janis. Jack feels guilty because he knows he contributed to the break-up of the marriage, yet he just can't forgive Janis for the affair and for leaving. Janis knows her own wrongdoing. But there is even more guilt. The children feel guilty because they think they contributed to the break-up, and Janis's girlfriend feels guilt over her role in the break-up.

No one from Janis's old church ever came by to see her and

Janis can't bring herself to return where she isn't wanted and where she would only be the center of gossip. In short, the former family had become dropouts from church.

Discussion

There are thousands of Janises and Jacks in our world. Guilt that remains unresolved prevents them from gaining a satisfactory resolution to their crises. People who have a breakdown in their relationship with God normally have other relational problems. Had both Janis and Jack been able to renew or establish a relationship with the Lord, they would have taken the first step in restoring their own relationship. When people resolve their guilt with God, they can better resolve guilt with others. When they know that God has forgiven them, they can feel as if they have Someone else giving them the strength necessary to forgive others and to be forgivable. If God can forgive them, then others can, too. This thought helps people receive forgiveness as it is given to them.

Some Christians believe they have committed the unforgivable sin or that they have sinned once too often. Non-Christians often feel they have been so rotten that God could never forgive them. People who feel this way should be directed to the encouragement of the Bible (John 3:16, 17; 1 John 1:9; Matt. 6:9–13; 18:21, 22; Luke 17:1–6). God is willing to forgive anyone's sins. First they must seek a relationship with Jesus Christ, the only Son of God. They must first confess that they are sinners, ask for forgiveness for their sins, and then ask Jesus to be their Lord. When they ask Jesus to be their Lord they are expressing their desire to do his will, to live as he wants them to. When they sin, Christians are in effect saying, "I don't want to do what you want me to do, Lord. I want to do it my way." Just as with a parent–child relationship, such an attitude causes a disruption in the relationship which needs to be restored if happiness is to return.

There are some steps that could have been taken that would have helped both Jack and Janis. In a counseling situation you might find these steps helpful:

1. Help the person identify the feeling of guilt and the cause of it.[5]

2. Help determine if it is guilt, coming from an emotional tendency to blame oneself for anything that goes wrong.

3. Help the person ask the Lord for forgiveness. (If the person is not a Christian, lead him or her to salvation.)

4. Explain that God has forgiven and help the person accept God's forgiveness. Guilt may have become a traveling companion that doesn't automatically disappear.

5. Explain the need for the person to ask injured or wronged parties for forgiveness, and, if possible, to make restitution.

6. Encourage the restoration of broken relationships and continual bridge-building.

7. Encourage the person to act as if he or she is forgiven and restored. Some people hold on to their guilt by acting guilty.

We who are Christians need to make sure that we are helpful toward persons going through the process of resolving guilt. If we are not forgiving, what kind of a model have we created for the person who is attempting to grow spiritually? If someone from Janis's church had attempted to help her through the pain and crisis of guilt, the final result might have been different.

There are several steps a caring Christian can take in helping those who are in spiritual crisis.

1. Go to the hurting person with an attitude that you could have been in the same spot. Do not go as the parent who is going to correct the child.

2. If the person is willing to talk about his or her guilt or hurt, hear the person out without being the judge. The person is probably being a pretty tough judge. Conviction is the task of the Holy Spirit, not of yourself.

3. Help the person to become aware of God's willingness to forgive. You might say that what he or she has done was not good, but it is forgivable.

4. Praying with a person who is seeking forgiveness is often very helpful and comforting.

5. Act as if the person is forgiven once forgiveness is requested.

6. Possibly you can help the person to restore relationships and/or make restitution to injured parties.

7. Encourage the person as he or she does things in a fashion that will create healing for self or others.

There are many types of events or experiences that can cause spiritual crisis. They usually are associated with a breakdown in the individual's relationship with God. The key to overcoming the crisis then is to restore the relationship between the person and God.

Common Feelings and Issues for Counselors to Address

- insecurity or panic from confusion of beliefs
- guilt (feels bad, dirty)
- need for restoration of relationship
- anger, toward God and others
- acceptance of God's forgiveness
- self-forgiveness
- acceptance from counselor

PART THREE

THE TECHNIQUES

IN THIS SECTION we would like to focus on specific crisis counseling techniques. Chapter 8 presents major techniques for use with those in a crisis. Chapters 9 and 10 discuss issues related to treatment, including prevention of crises and your own burnout and training of lay church leadership.

CHAPTER EIGHT

COUNSELING TECHNIQUES FOR CRISIS INTERVENTION

COUNSELORS NEED TO HAVE a grasp of techniques that have been developed specifically for crisis intervention.[1] With crisis counseling there are unique principles that would not apply in more general long-term counseling. As the following chart shows, crisis counseling is not simply a compact version of long-term counseling. Time is a major issue and a driving force in this process. The first seventy-two hours following a crisis are critical. What transpires during these hours will have a long-term impact.

Summary of Differences between Long-term Counseling and Crisis Counseling

Crisis	*Long-term*
Emotionally intensive	Less emotionally intensive
Goals: restore emotional equilibrium; problem resolution; deal with conscious	Goals: long-term growth; work through long-standing conflicts; deal with unconscious
Focus on immediate	Focus on past, present, future
Treatment modality: environmental manipulation; focus on feelings and action	Treatment modality: personal change; focus on introspection
Appointment any hour; undefined length	Often scheduled; for one hour
Directive; early confrontation of unrealistic perspectives and unproductive behavior	May be nondirective; exploratory; time for building rapport
No formal personality diagnosis[2]	Often has diagnosis of personality features
Use of many resource people	Primarily use of one counselor

We'll discuss the treatment in terms of both assessment and intervention. We realize that the moment you are contacted by a person who is in a crisis, your intervention has already begun, yet we will make these two distinctions to give some structure to the overall treatment process.

Assessment

One of the keys to effective crisis counseling is rapid and accurate assessment. One must quickly gain an understanding of the current situation, the emotional strengths of, and the resources available to the person experiencing the crisis. In the following outline we will summarize the major issues to be considered during assessment.

Assessment Checklist

I. The Precipitating Event
   A. What event has occurred recently?
   B. Is the situation getting better or worse?
   C. Are there cumulative events that make this the "final straw"?[3]
   D. Is the first event presented the real issue or is there a more stressful event in the background?

II. Perception
   A. What is the perceived danger to the person?
   B. What is the perceived loss?
   C. What unrealistic messages is the client giving him- or herself?[4]
   D. How does client see the event affecting his or her future?

III. Emotional Functioning
   A. What are the more salient emotions, i.e., fear, joy, anger?
   B. What is the history of ability to cope?
   C. Is the anxiety level preventing problem solving?
   D. Is he or she out of touch with reality?

IV. Behavior
   A. What has client attempted to do that has been ineffective?
   B. What has counselee attempted to do that has been effective?
   C. Are there responsibilities (such as the care of children) that are being ignored due to self-concern?

V. Internal Resources
   A. What is the level of personal strength in being able to cope?
   B. What evidence is there for spiritual strength or growth?
   C. What is the general health condition?

VI. External Resources
   A. What is the role of the family in the crisis and in its solution?
   B. Is the counselee in close touch with relatives who can help?

C. Is the counselee part of a social network? If so, who can be identified to help with each specific aspect?
D. Are there social agencies that can be brought in to help?

VII. Motivation for Help
A. How motivated is client to try new solutions?
B. What factors are preventing a solution?
C. Is there a sense of hope?
D. Does counselee simply blame others or does he or she feel corrective action is possible?

VIII. Potential Maladaptive Adjustment
A. Is client suicidal, potentially violent, or homicidal?
B. Is client likely to take drastic action that will be detrimental to self or others?
C. Is referral for medication or hospitalization necessary?
D. Is client making decisions that will have a major, long-term detrimental effect on his or her life?

First Things First

During the assessment process the counselor formulates general ideas and then moves quickly to substantiate them. One of the keys to effective assessment is to ask specific questions along with more general questions.[5] The general questions are good for broaching a new subject. For example, you might start with, "What brought you here to see me today?" Then, once an area of discussion has opened, you can and should get down to specifics. Ask direct questions, such as, "In this time of depression have you felt suicidal?" or "Who in your family could watch the children while you visit your husband in the hospital?"

In the assessment phase gather as much information as possible, even starting with your observation of the counselee as he or she enters the office. What is the person's emotional tone or level of intensity or disorganization? These can be noted by the way the person dresses, walks, looks, responds. When the factual information coincides with your observation, you'll feel somewhat satisfied that the puzzle pieces fit together. If these two are not in agreement, you may need to make a more extensive evaluation.

You'll want to be aware of the fact that some people are not immediately able to define the precipitating event. For example, a male counselee may only know that he is emotionally distressed. He may not yet realize what is prompting that response. You then need to explore what changes have occurred in the counselee's world of home, family, job, school. It is not possible to proceed without an accurate understanding of this person's perception. "Counsel in the heart of man is like deep water, But a man of understanding will draw it out" (Prov. 20:5).

Understanding the Counselee's Perception

Once an event has been identified and you feel comfortable that it is the major precipitating factor, you should work toward understanding how this event is perceived. As some authors have noted, the crisis does not lie directly in the event. The crisis is the result of the interaction between the person and the event.[6] The perception of the counselee and the kinds of messages given to self about the event produce the crisis. The mother who says to herself, *My children have all grown and left home; it is beautiful to see the progress in their lives,* will have a vastly different experience than the mother who thinks, *my children have all grown and left home; now I'll be lonely and I have no purpose left in life.*

The next step, then, is to clarify how counselees perceive the precipitating events. They may be giving themselves all kinds of unrealistic messages that would throw anybody into a crisis. For example, if a man asks a woman to return an engagement ring, she may well give herself many unrealistic messages about her future. Basically, these may boil down to *I will never be loved, accepted, nor happy again.*

Due to intense emotions, the person may be blinded to resources or possible solutions. As part of assessment, you, the counselor, need to gain information that will allow you to suggest creative resources or alternatives for action that the client has not considered.

Introductory psychology classes teach the flight or fight response during times of danger. When pressures build, we are inclined to flee or resist. This interferes with our efforts to regain equilibrium. You may identify possible productive action which has not been taken because the person is locked into a track of either flight or fight. The person may be moving through life fluctuating from one course to another, propelled only by a flood of emotion.

Before you offer a solution, it is critical that you assess the various resources within the life sphere of the person. Even though the client may be pushing early in the session for answers, you need to continue your evaluation until you have a completed picture of the event, perception, and resources.[7]

Proverbs gives us a good direction on this by stating, "He who answers a matter before he hears it, It is folly and shame to him" (18:13).

INTERVENTION

Assessment is the foundation for the plan of intervention. We, therefore, want to emphasize the importance of accuracy in spite of time pressures. Intervention in crisis counseling is generally thought of in terms of a short time frame. The first seventy-two hours after a crisis are critical, and crisis intervention is usually thought of as occurring over a four-to-six week span. By this time the crisis has either been resolved or matters have deteriorated to the point of hospitalization. The counselor must move quickly into intervention even during the first counseling session.

In his book *Christian Counseling*, Gary Collins adeptly notes several goals for crisis counseling. These should always serve as a background for intervention. They are summarized as follows:

1. Help the person return to his usual level of functioning; 2. decrease anxiety; 3. teach crisis-solving techniques; 4. teach biblical principles so the person grows as a result of the crisis.[8]

Intervention actually begins at the point of contact. Your availability and willingness to spend time with the person in crisis is already a part of intervention. In the rest of this chapter we'd like to present some specific principles that are crucial to crisis counseling.

See the Person Immediately

When you know of someone going through a crisis, even if you do nothing else, arrange to be with that person immediately. If you do not know what to do, that's okay. If you do not know what to say, that's okay.

People are better able to deal with pressure because of their interconnectedness with God and with others. This concept is emphasized in 1 Corinthians 12, and one gets a real sense of this connectedness from John 15:1–8. Jesus is stating that he is the Vine and that we have to be connected to him if we are going to bear fruit. He also tells us that without a connection to him we can do nothing. Interestingly, he talks about the bearing of fruit as the means to showing that we are disciples (v. 8). In this passage one cannot avoid the emphasis on love that comes through this interconnectedness. He summarizes in verse 17, saying, "These things I command you, that you love one another." The emphasis is this: People should be interconnected to each other by acts of love that are possible because these people are connected to Christ. This stands in direct contrast to the person who emphasizes emotional prowess by trying to go through a crisis alone, or the person who is facing a crisis alone because he or she doesn't have any close relationships.

First Corinthians 12:12–31 states that we are one body. Again, the emphasis is on relatedness to each other. In verses 15 and 16 Paul notes that a foot or ear that decides it doesn't need to be connected and declares itself as not a part of the body *is* still a part of the body, no matter what it says. Even more, the rest of the body goes on functioning as if the foot or ear is a part. In a crisis there is an intense need for this connectedness. Certainly you cannot force help on those who isolate themselves, but your offer should stand even though a person denies needing it.[9]

Jesus modeled this principle of immediacy. Matthew tells of a Roman soldier who came to him in a crisis; the man's servant was terribly ill. Jesus responded by saying, "I will come and heal him." He did not say, "Well, come back in a week or two. If he is not better . . ." or even, "I think I can come Thursday afternoon between 3:00 and 3:15." He said, "I will come." What immediate availability! Jesus was willing to drop everything and go. As it turned out, the soldier's faith was sufficient so that Jesus did not even need to see the servant to heal him.

Matthew 9:18, 19 shows us another example. A Jewish official whose daughter had just died came to Jesus. The Scriptures say, "So Jesus arose and followed him." Again he immediately responded to those in crisis. Certainly this was true time after time with those who needed him.

Just "being there" is also well illustrated by Job's friends. They weren't exactly the greatest resource people in the world, but they can be commended because they were willing to sit with Job during his afflictions. Job 2:12, 13 says that they came to be with him but didn't even speak for the first seven days. One must give them credit for coming and staying with him for that length of time. The overall principle of going quickly to be with those in crisis is probably the most important aspect of crisis ministry.

Talk with the Whole Family

Whenever one family member has a crisis, the whole family has a crisis. Therefore, if at all possible (at some early stage of intervention), see the whole family, not just one individual. Each person resides and lives in relationship to those around him or her; if one is impacted, all the rest of the system is impacted.

For example, you may talk to a boy who is very anxious and distressed, yet the underlying problems may not be his. His role in the family is that of symptom-bearer; when another person has a crisis, he is the one whose life demonstrates the crisis to the outside world. Mom and Dad have a terrible marriage which is headed for a separation crisis. They deal with their pressure by talking with friends or by drinking or by working more hours. Little Johnny, meanwhile, is ready to explode. He begins stealing from the store and manages to get caught. In subtle ways it is Johnny's role to misbehave when there is pressure in the family. This way of operating becomes the pattern for bringing family stress out into the open where Mom and Dad may attempt to deal with it. It would be a major mistake to counsel with just Johnny.[10]

In a similar fashion, different family members experience the same crisis differently and express it differently, but all are affected. Therefore, deal with the family as a system—if you want to be effective in helping them work through the crisis.[11]

Allow Expression of Feelings Within Limits

The third aspect then is to allow the person to talk about feelings. If there is a crisis, then there are plenty of feelings to be explored. It is very helpful for the counselee to be able to share these feelings with another person who understands, regardless of whether the listener agrees or disagrees with the perception presented.[12]

We suspect the grief of Job in the midst of crisis after crisis is about the deepest grief one could experience. He described it as heavier than the sand of the sea (Job 6:2, 3). In fact, the grief was so heavy Job wished he could lie down and die (Job 6:8, 9). He had hit bottom and was in the depths of despair.

When you see someone going through a crisis, the pain is visible. What do you do with the pain you see in the lives of others? Some people try to ignore it. Others try to wrestle it away from the person and carry it themselves. Some people try to convince the person in crisis that the crisis doesn't exist. Others try to minimize it or quickly eliminate it. Some people feel uncomfortable with it, so they look in the other direction. Jesus says, "Blessed are those who mourn, For they shall be comforted" (Matt. 5:4). Or another translation would be, "Happy are those who mourn." In short, it is all right to mourn. In fact, it can even lead to happiness. The principle then is this: When you help someone through a crisis, allow the person the opportunity to be anxious or to grieve. Do not take away from the counselee that which can be a meaningful and healing experience.

When in fact there has been a significant loss in one's life, one needs to set aside time to grieve. Recognize along with your client that rage, shame, or helplessness may flow deep inside and accompany the sense of grief. If the client has lost a person, the griever may want to spend some time visualizing a scene he or she had with the person who was lost and then say, "I will never have that experience again." The feelings of sadness and loss will no doubt follow. This then prepares the counselee for the new and for the opportunity to move ahead without all the baggage of repressed grief.

At some point you need to move the session beyond expression of emotion only and move into the problem and action. It is important to gain skill in sensing when to allow time for ventilation of emotion and when to allow time for dealing with cognitive issues. These two need to be placed in balance in crisis techniques. The way to keep this balance is to stay focused on the person, moving the session to meet his or her need.

Focus on the Here and Now

You may discover experiences earlier in the client's life or past events that contributed or led into this crisis. For example, perhaps you note that a major crisis is being precipitated because the person is facing a move to a new location. Maybe you note that as a child the client had moved but that the parents kept the information from the child until the day before the moving van arrived. This childhood event precipitated a crisis that left permanent scars.

It is easy to drift back into discussion of such former events and experiences that are in some way related to the current crisis. However, this becomes an easy substitute for dealing with the current crisis. Stay focused on the here and now. Even when a person is clearly affected by feelings left over from the past, remember that these feelings have been there for a long time. There will be time to deal with these after the current crisis begins to subside. Later, you may ask about these feelings that the crisis has elevated to the surface. However, during the time of the crisis, stay focused on the here and now.

What is happening now? What is the person experiencing? What is the client feeling? What is the client going to do about it? We are admonished to live in the present a day at a time. This is part of the wisdom of the ages.

Define the Problem and Clarify the Client's Perception of It

When a person comes seeking relief from anxiety, lack of appetite, sleeplessness, and so forth, you need to define the crisis rapidly. Identify the event that has recently happened or that seems imminent. What event does this person perceive as a threat? What does the counselee perceive to be threatened—self-worth, acceptance, role mastery?

Usually it is best not to argue with a person who feels something is a crisis, even if you do not see it as such. However, you can help to clarify various points and perceptions by sharing your feelings and perceptions and by asking questions. For example, a woman who has suffered a financial loss may be telling herself that others will no longer care about her, that she will always be in debt, or that life will forevermore be drudgery. These statements that are producing depression may need to be challenged, not in a combative way, but by providing definite and clear alternative positions that are not presented in argumentative fashion. You are not trying to win a court case. You are trying to help her clarify ideas and rethink conclusions.

Many people in crisis may well breathe sighs of relief when you clearly identify specific events or hazards that precipitated their crises.[13] It is helpful for them to have feedback as to the exact problem they are confronting. This gives them a starting point.

Clarify Reality

After you have defined the crisis it is important for you to state clearly their perceptions. Clarify reality as you see it without arguing with them about what is and is not reality. If counselees refuse to see reality, you have a measure of the depth of their feelings about the crises. This tells you of the importance of the issues in their lives. You will need to consider spending more time talking further about the issues or possibly referring the person to a counselor with more training than yourself.

One's distortion may veer off in one of two directions: unrealistic optimism that includes denial of part of the problem or unrealistic pessimism in assessment of the crisis and/or of the outcome. Unrealistic optimism may be a defense mechanism that is helping the client cope with the pain of the crisis. You do not want to be like a bull in the china shop and destroy the client's sense of hope or coping. It takes great sensitivity to support the person while gently pointing out reality. Here we think of the husband whose wife of many years was dying of cancer. In her final stages he still wanted her to be doing housework and preparing meals. He was suffering extreme loss in his crisis. He desperately wanted her to be well, when in fact she was not well. He needed to be understood, but he also needed to accept the reality of her condition.

More often, people are unrealistically pessimistic. The boss was unhappy about a job she had completed and it threw her into a crisis. She had told herself she was going to be fired and that she would never get another job. In reality, the boss liked most of her work and would not have considered firing her. If her job were in jeopardy, she had outstanding skills with which she could get another position. In her crisis she needed someone to ask her if the boss had actually threatened the loss of her job. If so, how soon? What had she done prior to this job? What skills had she acquired, etc.? Soon the questions should lead her to a more realistic perception and should help dissipate the crisis.

Point Out Disruptive Behaviors and Alternatives

When helping someone through a crisis, it is useful to point out any ineffective behaviors he or she is using to cope with the crisis. The person may be attempting all sorts of behaviors that are either causing more problems or are wasting time and energy that could be used constructively.

They were in their mid-forties and had lived in the same neighborhood for fourteen years. He had been with the current company for nine years, and she was enjoying the new job she'd taken once the youngest child was in school. There were fewer financial pressures now, and their lives were settled and going along well. One evening their eighteen-year-old daughter told them she wanted to talk with both of them. This had never happened before, and they knew by her tone and appearance something major was on her mind. The air filled with tension and apprehension as they solemnly took seats in the living room. Their model child who was also a good student explained to them that she was pregnant. The shock of the crisis hit them both. The father was hurt, angry, disappointed and frustrated all at the same time. He handled it by hitting the ceiling. He yelled, he shouted, paced the floor, and blamed her. Hadn't she been taught better? What had she done with her life? He decided quickly that she must move out of the house and away from home. He wanted her out! Only later, after considerable discussion, was this rapid solution seen as perhaps making the crisis for the family worse, not better. His daughter did not need more rejection at this point in time. Kicking her out of the house was not solving the many complex issues that faced the family. Likewise, she was not prepared to make the many decisions in front of her without the assistance and support of her family.

If the crisis is not rapidly relieved, the person often becomes confused and less effective in arriving at a solution. At the point of dysfunction one needs encouragement to move away from ineffective behaviors and toward behaviors that are effective. The Prodigal Son was apparently in a crisis when he ran out of money in a land that was experiencing a famine. He had tried reckless living; now he tried caring for pigs that ate better than he—or at least he perceived himself as starving. The Bible says that finally he came to his senses (Luke 15:17). He decided to go home and confess to his father and ask forgiveness. The other strategies were ineffective—not working.

This is so often the case with those going through a crisis. One is under great pressure to reestablish equilibrium. The client wants out from under the distress and will grasp at straws. Clients may move quickly to do things that may hurt themselves or complicate the issues because they don't think through the long-term implications of the behavior. Therefore, when you work with a person who is in a crisis you need to think carefully about this behavior and solutions. Examination of solutions can be a very loving act. Since you are not under the same pressure, you can provide for clients a perspective they may have difficulty providing for themselves.

Do not accept at face value the client's plans or predictions about the results of plans. Weigh carefully the outcome of a selected course of behavior to determine if you are as optimistic as the client about the results. If you see pitfalls the person has not seen, these need to be highlighted.

Distorted predictions are especially prevalent in marital separations. A typical pattern is that the wife moves out and the husband is in a crisis. To deal with the crisis, he calls the wife daily and quotes her carefully selected scriptural admonitions. If he uses verses on love, they are mostly oriented to how she should be loving him more. This solution essentially causes more pressure and guilt and is designed to force her back. If this doesn't get an immediate response, he threatens to tell her parents about something terrible she has done. Usually he cannot get her back by guilt and, even if he does, he cannot rebuild a solid marriage on that foundation. In his desperation to solve his crisis, he drives her further away than she was before. Such a man needs help in assessing the methods he is using to relieve his painful crisis.

Part of the problem in a crisis is that the counselee does not see any alternatives. He or she may be so blocked by emotion that he or she cannot creatively consider alternatives. Questions, such as, "Have you thought about trying——," can be useful once you have thoroughly explored all the ineffective behaviors the client has tried. Some alternatives may have been too quickly eliminated because of mistaken perceptions about their feasibility or outcome. Therefore, you should carefully explore why the counselee thinks a possible alternative would not work, when that alternative seems viable to you.

Define Goals and Plan of Action

One of the most valuable contributions to people in crisis is to move them into action. The energy generated by a crisis can be channeled into a plan. As a rule of thumb, no matter what the crisis, try to help the person develop a plan of action. The client who actually does something to remedy the situation can begin to gain some relief. The person should have some clearly defined, specific, and attainable goals. If the crisis is a positive one, as the sudden responsibility that comes from inheriting a large sum of money from an unknown uncle, the client could begin to act by checking with several bankers about reputable financial advisors. If the counselee has suddenly lost a friend, the person may need to develop a plan for filling some of the empty days and eventually develop a plan for meeting new people (including specific places to go or functions to attend).

As people slowly and perhaps grimly take scoop shovels and clean the rubble of their home or pile up the pieces of charred furniture, their efforts fuel the adjustment process. Help the person in crisis to do something—even if it is a minor act. A small step is better than no step at all. If the counselee is depressed he or she may not feel like doing anything. But that feeling itself is a signal that the person *should* do something. The healing that comes from action needs to be recognized and encouraged. In some cases you may even have to go and help yourself so that the counselee can get started. That behavior on your part may provide the impetus one needs to begin. Jesus often had people do something as a demonstration of their faith. He told the lame to take up their beds and walk (Mark 2:11) and others to cast their nets out farther from shore (Luke 5:4). Perhaps as people begin doing something, they begin to renew their faith and their hope. Perhaps it is the renewed hope that brings relief from the crisis.

Clarify Expectations

It is usually helpful for a client to clarify what he or she expects from you. Some people seek help with a crisis without having thought much about what they expect. Some people expect you to listen and support them. Some people expect you to help them in a specific way, and others expect you to take over their crises and solve them. Some will view you as the omniscient parent figure who can soothe away any hurt. There are a variety of ideas concerning what is anticipated from both the helper and the person in the crisis. When the expectations are clarified, all parties involved will come through the experience with better understanding. Tell the person what you as a helper are willing and able to do and not do. Ask yourself what the counselee is wanting from you. If you give it, will it help or hinder adjustment or foster too much dependency? Ask the counselee about expectations of you. How does the counselee perceive you as being helpful? It is virtually never helpful for you to take upon yourself the counselee's crisis, and if that is an expectation, you should discuss your human limitations.

Here we think of the ministry of the Holy Spirit who, among other things, brings comfort. His ministry is that of one who comes alongside to help. He does not remove the situation but rather helps us through it. The model of coming alongside to help is a good concept from which to base your expectations about what you will do and what you anticipate from the counselee. Of course, your expectations will vary with the person, the situation, and the person's current level of functioning within the crisis. At one point you may be willing to do a lot more for the person than you would be willing to do at a later time. It would be inappropriate to ask a lot from a person who just lost a spouse. But that same person a week later could well be at a very different point.

The principle should be to assist, but not to do something one could do for oneself. Even if you somehow could take on another's crisis, it would not be fair to that person. The counselee needs to work through the process, not just be rescued from pain.

Generate Hope

"Hope deferred makes the heart sick" (Prov. 13:12 NIV). It is easy to forget the immeasurable power of hope in a person's life. Without hope, motivation and drive soon are replaced with apathy and discouragement. If there is any reasonable cause for hope in a situation, it is helpful to convey the expectation of a successful outcome. When hope is gone, the counselee may need you to provide it. At the same time, you do not want to convey a false sense of hope.

Virtually every crisis includes some aspect that can be spotlighted so as to stimulate encouragement. The baseball player who loses partial function of his arm needs to know his baseball days are over. He also needs to know that it is not the end of his happiness. It may not even be the end of his involvement in baseball. Perhaps he could coach or manage a team or, if he has another occupation, he might coach Little League. People need specific ideas upon which they can focus. The lack of hope comes often from generalizations. It is not that they tell themselves, ***I'll never again be able to participate in baseball,*** or ***I'll miss my friend.*** It is more like, ***I'll never be happy again; my purpose for life is over.*** Those in crisis need reassurance that things will ultimately be all right, that they can be happy again. Norman Wright has noted different forms of reassurance that can be helpful. He states that assurances ("The problem is common and resolution is possible"; "Something can be done about it"; "You are not going insane"; "You will need to deal with relapse") can be very helpful.[14]

Present a view of the crisis that can generate positive concepts. Help the client look not only at the present state of crisis, but also far into the future.

When the crisis itself looks overwhelming, a light at the end of the tunnel can be lifesaving. People are able to accept a lot of difficulty if they know it will end—or even if they hope it will end. The crisis will not last forever.

If you can foresee positive aspects or indications of the termination of distress, point them out to the person who is struggling for hope. Your confidence that the outcome will be positive can be a valuable part of the process as long as it is specific and not presented as a pat-on-the-head cliché. Clichés usually only make things worse.

Utilize Additional Resources

As part of dealing with the crisis, pull into action all those you can think of who can offer support. A network of people helpers is a powerful resource. A person in a crisis often feels isolated and concerned about acceptance of others. The sheer number of people whom you can bring in to aid is an effective antidote to both of these factors.[15]

Do not try to be the hero and walk a client through the crisis alone. Utilize all others who can reasonably make a contribution. Someone going through a crisis is like an empty pail of water. Even if you contribute many cups full of water, you may have difficulty filling the pail by yourself. Even if you are multi-talented, you will have some areas where others are more capable or gifted.

One of the first considerations may be to decide if the counselee has his or her own social network that could be utilized to give support and strength at a time of crisis.[16]

Frequently, the person in crisis has already developed a network which simply needs to be activated. When you don't know all a person's significant others, you can ask who he or she would like to be with, providing that person is available.

Studies have indicated that the use of networks is effective in family therapy, rehabilitation settings, substance abuse, juvenile delinquency, personal problems, and marital discord.[17] Your job includes helping the counselee identify people with whom he or she has had contact in the past year. The listing could be by groupings, such as immediate and extended family, neighbors and friends, work associates, recreational friends, religious friends, doctors, teachers.[18] Network members can be used as resources, assisting you with planning, information gathering, and goal setting when the person in crisis cannot help him- or herself.

The first social group to turn to for the development of a support network is the individual's family. Mother, dad, brothers, sisters, aunts, uncles, cousins, in-laws, grandparents, and so forth can be of great help in dealing with crises. In the situation where someone needs to be with the person in crisis at all times, the family members can take turns.

Sometimes family members are not a good resource. When someone in the family is part of the problem, he or she will not work as an effective resource. For example, if a family member is attempting suicide, there may be someone in the family (or several members) contributing to the crisis. It is clear that such a family member would not be one to be intensely involved with the suicidal person's care. While those who use the family systems' approach may recognize the value of the entire family being involved, this does not suggest that all family members are a good resource at all times.

A valuable way to develop the family into a future resource in crises is to make available advance training. In churches, schools, or community organizations, families can be trained to become more effective, especially in crisis.

In addition to family and friends, the church can provide a

support network. This is especially needful in our culture, where so many people live a long distance from their families. The diversity found among church members makes it an invaluable resource. Father figures, mother figures, and supportive friends are often available. Often pastors, youth leaders, Sunday school teachers, and other church leaders will have an idea who would be of greatest help in dealing with a crisis.

You should also ask yourself whom you know who would be a willing resource. Perhaps the crisis requires someone who can manage money or time. Perhaps you know an administrator who could help the person. Maybe the client needs some leads on jobs and you know someone who has influence in hiring.

Sometimes you can think of a person who successfully came through a similar crisis. This person may be very valuable as a model or as a resource person who can suggest coping skills and provide hope. You need to be sure this person would not propose his or her solution as the only one, as no two situations are exactly the same. A person who has been through a similar crisis usually has high credibility to a person in crisis. In fact, we are taught that one of the purposes for which we suffer is so that we in turn may be able to help others through similar difficulties.

First Peter 1:6, 7 states, ". . . now for a little while, if need be, you have been grieved by various trials, that the genuineness of your faith . . . may be found to praise, honor and glory at the revelation of Jesus Christ." The greatest resource in most crises is caring people. Support networks can be developed for nearly all people in crisis.

There is a very important responsibility that a counselor must keep in mind: confidentiality. Sometimes many people knowing of someone's plight only contributes to the crisis. When approaching others to help, it is best to describe the problem, the need, and the type of person needing help. If the resource person then agrees to help, he or she should be informed of the responsibility as it relates to confidentiality.

Your skill as a crisis counselor involves more than knowing and using counseling techniques. It involves identifying additional resources, including social agencies and other professionals. Someone who is involved in crisis intervention is somewhat like a chef. A counselor pulls specific services from a variety of agencies and mixes them in proper proportions to create a unique mixture that applies to a specific person who is in a unique situation.

To be able to develop a resource and support system around a person in crisis the counselor must have done his or her homework before the crisis. A counselor needs to know what resources are available, their eligibility requirements and conditions for use, and their contact persons and methods.

Most counselors keep a resource file or index for which they can quickly reach. If a person in the midst of a crisis arrives at the office, it is awkward, time consuming, and ineffective for you to begin calling around in order to discover available social services. Also helpful is a current directory of social services. Nearly every community publishes such a yellow-pages-type listing of all local social service agencies. These can usually be purchased through the local United Way agency. The directory will give basic information about offered services but does not discuss the competency of the organization nor its basic philosophy.

Churches might develop a resource index and keep it at a central resource center where members can access it.

In developing a resource list, it is important to keep in mind that resource people and organizations move, change phone numbers, cease to provide services, add new services, or change their policies. It is critical to keep the resource list up-to-date by verifying your information every six months to a year.

Organizations that frequently deal with crises can be of particular help in developing a crisis resource list. You might check the following places for more information: hospital emergency rooms; police and fire departments; state, county, or city departments of social or human services; departments of employment; departments of mental health; and schools and colleges. Many communities have a community services or United Way director who can be a valuable base for development of a more comprehensive list.

A number of national professional organizations have lists of members who are qualified as resource persons in a crisis.

Many of these organizations will respond to an inquiry by giving you names and addresses of local association members. Of course you'll want to verify such information and, if possible, meet any persons you plan to use as a resource. You might want to ask yourself whether or not you would want to get help from this person. Due to professional ethics, most resource people cannot give you a list of satisfied clients. You can ask people who you know have faced a crisis if they can recommend individuals or organizations to you.

Sometimes the philosophy of an organization or the bias of a resource individual is contrary to your own world view or the view of those you hope to help. It is wise to know as much about resource groups, organizations, and people as possible. Many organizations have a pamphlet or a sheet that describes what they do and their philosophy.

Some organizations may, on the surface, appear to meet the need of a person in crisis, but they do so in such a way as to create another, possibly even greater, crisis. For example, an organization that advocates "free sex" (that is not likely to be mentioned in any literature) could produce yet another crisis in a person with moral values. The compounding of crises will no doubt extend the amount of time needed for resolution and recovery.

This resource "homework" will make you better prepared to get clients the help they need. Generally crisis-situation referrals are handled differently than other referrals. Crisis referrals may require much more direct involvement of the counselor. In crisis situations the counselor must make sure those needing referral actually arrive at the referral agency in a reasonable time frame. If referrals are necessary, sometimes the best way to help a person in crisis is to take him or her to the resource person or organization. As an example, if someone is in an emotional crisis that calls for hospitalization, it is best to accompany the person to the hospital. Even though in most cases confinement must be voluntary, your willingness to go with the person can give courage and, most important, the assurance that someone cares. If hospital confinement takes place, it is important for the support person to visit the patient regularly, as often as it is realistically possible.

Going with the person in crisis to an inpatient treatment facility says several things to that person: You are not alone. You are cared for, and I will help you until you are ready to get back on your own feet. Always remember that your ultimate goal is to help people in crisis *only* until they can get back on their own feet.

When you cannot take someone to a resource, a family member or friend can be enlisted to help. If for some reason the client goes on his or her own, call to make sure the individual arrived. If the person does not arrive, follow up and see what happened. Sometimes people do not arrive at resource centers because in their turbulence they have not understood directions, locations, or times of appointment. Or they may have changed their minds.

Most counselors have experienced frustration in not gaining feedback from agencies or professionals to which they've referred clients. One way of gaining feedback is by asking the counselee to sign a "release of information form." Such a form or letter is dated and signed by the adult person, or parent/guardian for minors, and states that you and the agency or professional may release information to each other. Such a procedure allows for follow-up which you may have to initiate. As agencies and individual professionals come to know you, greater cooperation and communication generally takes place.

Yet other resources are in written form, such as information on a specific timely topic. For example, if a person is suddenly unemployed, he or she may need information on how to apply for unemployment benefits. If the birth of a new child creates family stress, a couple/mother may benefit from a good book on the topic.

In the depth of a crisis some people will not want to read; others may find comfort in the written information and the act of "researching" possible solutions. You may want to develop a lending library that covers various topics. You'll want some of the books to present a biblical perspective and world view. The government publishes an array of topical booklets which can be purchased through the government printing office at minimal cost.

Many social agencies have free booklets on specific topics relating to the services they provide. It is important to screen such information to know which booklets or books to recommend.

Stay Flexible

There are principles for helping with a crisis, but every situation and person is so unique that there are no fixed rules or fixed solutions. It is important to understand the person's problems and feelings. From there on you want to stay as flexible as possible and utilize any reasonable strategy that will work. Be as creative as possible in thinking about support systems and plans of action. If the counselee's house burned down maybe the counselee can live with you for a while. Maybe there is a relative with whom the person could live. Maybe the person could house sit. Maybe you know of a vacant apartment. Maybe a garage could be fixed into temporary living quarters. Maybe you know of financial assistance on a new house. The possibility of solutions is limited only by your own and others' creative and inventive skills. There are innumerable solutions, some better than others, for that particular person, in that particular circumstance.

It is useful to glean possible solutions tried by others who went through similar situations, so long as this does not stymie your creativity. You do not want to look only into old solutions that may have fit well into different situations. Be courageous in attempting new and well-thought-out possibilities.

In Luke 9:10–17, Jesus decided to resolve a minor crisis for a crowd of five thousand who had nothing to eat. (Perhaps the more hungry ones would not have considered it a minor crisis.) His solution was to take the resources available (five loaves and two fishes) and bless them in order to meet the need. I think this causes us to ask a question: What resources are available that may be blessed and thereby become sufficient to meet the need? Certainly we want to be aware of what is available while remembering that ultimately its effectiveness depends on God. Proverbs 21:31 is a wonderful verse: "The horse is prepared for the day of battle, But deliverance is of the LORD."

Plan for a Follow-up

During the initial session it is important to conclude with a definitive plan for when you and the counselee can get back together again for another meeting. It is best if this is scheduled and carefully planned in terms of issues to be discussed. The counselee will then be able to look forward to and emotionally prepare for the meeting. There is usually a sense of relief to know that a helper will remain through the time of trial. It is important not to drop out of the picture during a time of crisis. Our greatest example of this comforting assurance is found in Hebrews 13:5, "For He Himself has said, 'I will never leave you, nor forsake you.'"

Sometimes people who go through crises place high expectations on themselves in terms of the effects of the crises. A week after a crisis has occurred, a counselee may wonder why the effects of the crisis are still so intense. A counselee who has lost a loved one may note that it still seems as if the deceased were in the other room. Although a counselee readily forgives others, he or she may not be able to let go of resentment toward a boss who handed out a pink slip. A counselee may not believe he or she actually retired; it seems like every day is Saturday. Such people need to be encouraged not to anticipate a balanced equilibrium within forty-eight hours. A few weeks later they should still have some of the residual feelings. A person should not be contributing to the emotional upheaval by condemning self for not having moved beyond the crisis during the first twenty-four hours.

Recently I talked on the phone with a friend who had been roughed up and robbed one night about a week and a half earlier. She was condemning herself for being fearful when going out at night. A strong Christian, she wondered where her faith was. Shouldn't she depend on the Lord's protection? She was telling herself that all uncomfortable feelings should not continue beyond a couple of days. Sometimes self-imposed spiritual expectations only add more weight to an already difficult crisis.

I would have felt something to be wrong if she had *not* been fearful. When one goes through a trauma like this, some element of fear should last a while. We are created to have emotions. It is part of our basic design. Sometimes emotions swell up apart from any apparent stimulus, and then we should question them. But when there has been a trauma to stimulate them, emotions should be expected. The Bible encourages us to deal with our feelings, not to deny or repress them.

People who are within a few weeks of a crisis event are still in the process of adjusting to the crisis. They need to be encouraged not to expect a cessation of feelings immediately. The most realistic expectation is a gradual tapering off of feelings with temporary increases around certain events or days. For example, if you lose a loved one, the loss will fade over time, except the pain may be more intense around that person's birthday, Christmas, or your anniversary. Eventually even these days will be less intense, although the remembrance will be there.

During the second or follow-up session it is important to review with the client any gains you have noted. This crisis technique gives encouragement that will tend to perpetuate the healing process. These gains may be only minor, but they need to be highlighted and elevated so as to give hope, that invaluable medicine.

CHAPTER NINE

PREVENTION OF CRISES

"IT'S NOT MY FAULT I couldn't handle my husband's walking out on me. He just did it and I couldn't help myself. I just fell apart." As Alice sat in my office telling her life story I found that I kept asking myself questions. How could her story have been different? Could she have avoided the way she interacted with her husband all these years? Would there have been new crises if she had responded differently to previous early crises?

If the crisis-producing event had been an earthquake or a war, certainly Alice wouldn't have had any influence on the event. But some stressful events are preventable; the breakup of Alice's marriage might have been one of them.

In what circumstances can one prevent a crisis? We recognize that a crisis is not only an event, it is also an inability to deal with one or more events. We effectively handle many stress-producing events each day. They become a crisis only when our coping mechanisms don't quickly bring us to equilibrium. In other words, when our coping mechanisms fail, a crisis follows.

Events that overtax our coping abilities can sometimes be prevented or prepared for in such a way as to decrease our stress. Prevention can take place if diversion and education are available. In this case diversion involves anticipating and taking steps to avoid the onset of the event; if the problem event has already started, steps can be taken to prevent its escalation. The second key is preventive education. It involves teaching people how to cope with stress and to manage crisis events.[1]

Crises can be prevented!

In this chapter we will discuss the *why* of prevention, early warning signals of a potential crisis, inner strength development, building supportive relationships, and management of environmental factors that cause crisis-producing stress. We'll conclude the chapter by discussing prevention of the crisis to which counselors are so vulnerable: burnout.

Why Prevention?

On the surface, it may seem obvious that prevention is necessary and important, but we see a minimal number of crisis prevention and preparation programs. At least we see few programs that state prevention and preparation as their goals.

If we look at the potential cost of crises, we gain a view of what prevention might help preserve. In extreme circumstances the result of human crisis can be suicide. T. M. Johnson has said that "for the victim suicide provides the sufficient solution to the problem."[2] The problem is often a crisis that becomes acute as a result of an intensifying event that compounds a chronic problem.

In one recent year, the U.S. Census figures revealed that 27,300 suicide attempts were successful.[3] According to Farberow, there are about fifty thousand direct suicide deaths each year plus forty times that many self-caused unintentional deaths.[4] Self-destructive behavior is a very serious problem in our society. If people, including those in our churches, could learn how to manage life events in more effective ways, it would seem that extreme stress could be avoided. While there are no data that can predict the number of lost lives that could be saved from self-destructive behavior, it seems that the number could be significant.

In less intensive situations, crises also "cost" in terms of emotional distress and agony. Suffering can sometimes serve a purpose, but often unnecessary suffering can lead to fears and dysfunction and the interruption of relationships. When under undue pressure, people are often less effective in reaching out to others emotionally and spiritually; they are too preoccupied with inner needs.

The cost may also be in terms of physical problems as well as emotional and spiritual loss. Medical problems have a way of cropping up at times of high stress. Still another cost can be financial, due to loss of time from productive activity or cost of professional care. Time spent coping with crisis is also time lost from personal growth-producing activities. The person's energy is being drained trying to regain equilibrium instead of reaching toward self-actualization.

From many perspectives, it becomes clear that we need to consider the ultimate value of prevention. But why have so few resources been put into prevention? There are several apparent reasons. First, some people have a misperception—that crisis events cannot be prevented. They assume that if a crisis is going to happen, it will happen; nothing can be done about it.

Second, people tend to have excellent 20-20 vision—by hindsight. But their foresight is much muddier. Sometimes people do not prepare for prevention because they do not see a potential crisis before it hits them. If you suspected that a crisis-producing situation was about to confront you, you would no doubt take preventive action. You would drive more defensively if you knew someone might plow into your car today, but since it ordinarily doesn't happen, you tend to grow lax.

Several months ago I was on the freeway when I saw what appeared to be a drunk driver swerving all over the freeway. I stayed way back even though that meant driving way below the speed limit. I wanted to avoid a crisis-producing situation. Dozens of other drivers responded the same way, but often crises come upon us unawares.

Third, people don't practice prevention because they think crises are not going to happen to them. We've long ago lost count of the number of husbands who have come to us and said, "I never felt my wife would leave me. I thought we had a good marriage. I felt it only happened to people who aren't Christians." If people feel crises happen only to "the other guy," they have nothing to prepare for or prevent.

Fourth, many people don't have any idea of what help is available for preventing crises. Yet a great deal of prevention information is available all around them. They simply may not identify it as such or they may not know how to access the information. When researching this book at the library of the local university, that has nearly twenty thousand students, I was startled to note that some of the books on crisis had been checked out only about twenty times over a decade. Many organizations, such as the Red Cross, have materials on crisis prevention, but only a fraction of the population takes advantage of this literature which often is free.

Fifth, prevention does not become a part of a potential victim's life because there are not convenient courses, seminars, or training programs. There are exceptions to this, but these are few in number. Most churches have not developed programs for this purpose. Public agencies offer some prevention programs but most are rather narrow in scope, such as crime-prevention programs by the police.

Finally, prevention is not practiced because of economic concerns. Most of our financial resources are used to pay for immediate needs and they are not set aside for prevention. The wisdom of the proverb "an ounce of prevention is worth a pound of cure" seems pushed aside in real life. However, prevention is surely a wiser use of resources.

Early Warning Signals

"Face it, Allison is just accident prone," declared Alex (in utter frustration) after Allison had just had her sixth accident at work in less than three years. Alex's boss, Mildred, responded, "Alex, either Allison finds another job or she goes to the company's accident-prevention school. We just can't continue to pay for her being prone to these very costly accidents." This scene is repeated in many company and governmental agencies. Employers and insurance companies have learned that an investment in prevention can pay large dividends.

While much personal growth comes about as a result of a crisis experience, repeated crises produce chronically dysfunctional behavior. In the latter case, the cost can be very high.

You need to become alert and spot people who are "crisis prone" or who are entering into a potential crisis situation. You need to be attuned to patterns and potential situations.

When these events take place with no apparent warning, there is little that can be done to prepare support for the person experiencing the crisis. When a crisis hits, support must be developed immediately and often it is not nearly as complete or effective as when warning signals of the impending events were apparent. Frequently, a pastor or counselor or other person close to an individual can analyze some developing events to foresee an impending crisis.

Some early warning signals may be more apparent to a third party than to a family member or to the person who will face the coming crisis.

Norman is forty-five, overweight by about fifty pounds, has smoked several packs of cigarettes a day until recently, seldom exercises, has taken no vacations, is very defensive about himself, and comes from a family where heart attacks have been common. Would anyone be shocked if Norman fell over dead one day? Yes, probably his wife would be. She feels she could not face life without Norman; so in an unrealistic attempt to avoid the potential problem she has closed her eyes to his being at risk. She hopes maybe denial will work as a preventative. Many a pastor could sit down and make a list of high-risk parishioners. These people may then be informally encouraged in directions that will begin to minimize the risk. The pastor may serve as a shepherd that is alert to potential risk.

The Sunday school coordinator, Nora, comes into the pastor's office one day to talk about problems she is having with several teachers in the nursery department. In the course of her discussion she shares that her husband has been working a lot of overtime and she just has not had time to do all the work a coordinator should do. The pastor gives her encouragement and a few suggestions on dealing with the problems she faces. Within the week the youth sponsor lets the pastor know that Nora's oldest child has been a real problem for the last month or so. Nora's husband has not been to church for over two months. Nora gives the excuse that he is just so exhausted because of the extra ten-to-fifteen hours of overtime every week.

You have no doubt already spotted the warning signals of changed behavior, children acting out, distancing, and so forth. A pastor is in a unique situation: With dozens of families to shepherd and possible time lapses between interactions of weeks and months, it is difficult to analyze events, families, and behaviors so as to see a series of events that indicates the existence of a problem, such as with Nora.

A number of signals can be a tip-off that a problem is developing, including:

1. change in church attendance (more or less)
2. change in attention span (appears to be daydreaming or in another world)
3. change in style of living:
   a. change in eating patterns (overeating constantly or stopping eating altogether)
   b. increase in or onset of drinking or drug use
   c. unkempt appearance or sudden concern for perfection
   d. growing obsession with or repulsion for sexual matters
   e. change in sleep patterns
   f. sudden changes in spending patterns
4. change in social relationships
   a. increase in antisocial behavior
   b. increase in argumentative spirit, even with old friends
   c. marked increase in dependence
   d. increase in critical nature
   e. marked increase in home conflicts
   f. withdrawal from family

5. change in work functioning
   a. sudden resignation from jobs or decrease in job performance
   b. increase in altercations with co-workers
   c. loss of creativity
   d. more frequent "silly" accidents on the job

Sudden or fairly rapid change in a person is generally the very signal that something significant is going on in the person's life. When these signals begin to take place, especially when there is a pattern of them, it is time to begin to assess more definitively the stress in that person's life. A crisis may be brewing.

There are a couple of factors to take into account in being sensitive to potential crises in a person's life. Consider their resources. People who have limited inner strength or supportive relationships (such as few close, personal friends)[5] and/or limited spiritual resources tend to have a lower level of coping skills. They are more vulnerable to stress and to crisis. Intensity, severity, and/or frequency of the stressors impacting the individuals also need consideration.

Prevention of Crisis by Strengthening Relationships

Building a Relationship with Oneself

"I feel like all I am inside is a little green pea," lamented one client during a counseling session. Many people feel insignificant. They just don't feel as if there's much inside of them; they just aren't worth much. It could be concluded that such people don't have very much in the way of inner strength.

Heintz Kohut declares that self-preservation is the motive for all a person's defenses.[6] If people deny the world is falling down around them, they are attempting to cope with what would be more than they could handle. They are preserving a self-concept that says they are able to deal with their world. This can be seen in the case of the engineer who is laid off and just goes home and waits for weeks, even months, for a call to return to work. Denial is a way of dealing with inner anxiety which has been heightened by the crisis.

For some Christians, building up inner strength and emotional resources may seem counter to trusting in God. We however do not think emotional development is in some way unspiritual. The words of C. S. Evans may be helpful here. "Psychology that is Christian must be psychology that makes room for the concept of the self and related concepts such as belief, desire, meaningful action, responsibility, and interaction."[7] Building self-worth may be a matter of people learning to accept the skills and abilities God has given them and learning the meaning of *grace;* they are accepted even though they are not perfect. Self-acceptance does not mean they attempt to function apart from trust in God.

Frank was very shy. He said little during his first counseling session. Often he looked down, never directly at his counselor. He was a young man who saw himself as "no good." His mother repeatedly redid everything he had done, down to the simplest things. Frank clearly heard the message that he could do nothing right. His father was more direct; he just kept telling Frank that he was "stupid" and had "nothing worth saying." Frank saw himself as a worm and played the role to the hilt.

Frank had a lot of negative feelings about himself. He felt he should not speak up because he would only reveal just how "useless" he was. After a period of developing some trust in his counselor, Frank began to talk about himself, although very carefully at first. He wanted to know if a counselor would reject him. As the weeks went by, he realized that no matter how hard he tried he could not get the counselor to reject him. Over the months Frank began to find that the counselor respected him as a person. As a matter of fact, he felt accepted. He began to find out that he could be "himself" and be liked. In time, he began to feel good about himself a great deal of the time.

During therapy, the counselor encouraged Frank to test out his skills, abilities, and gifts. When things did not go right, the counselor helped Frank see that he was learning something new, like riding a bicycle for the first time. Perfection wasn't expected. As problems arose in various situations, Frank began to attempt to solve them instead of hiding from them. Most of the time, solutions he attempted worked as he began to see that he could solve problems. Before long Frank was ready to take quite a big step for him. He wanted to get a better job. With the counselor's help, he developed a "plan of action." In a short period of time, Frank had a new job that paid more than any he'd ever had before. As a result of the increased income, he made another plan which he carried out; he got a better apartment.

Frank has been promoted two times in the past year and now drives a new car. He's still fairly quiet and yet he now knows he can do many things well and he believes he can accomplish most of his goals. He has a new sense of inner strength. When confronted with stressful situations that could become a crisis, he believes enough in his own ability that he sits down to work out solutions with regular success. One of the best measures of his developing self-esteem is that when a solution fails he does not give up; rather, he tries again. He is able to more effectively minister to others. Recently he helped his local church build a new playground. He is much better prepared to deal with future crises because of an inner change of self-concept. A key to prevention of crisis is to help the individual have a realistic and positive self-esteem before a potential crisis develops.

Building Relationships with Others

Every human being needs a social support system. This is especially true in the face of crisis.[8]

The individual who slips into social isolation is one whose social anxiety has overwhelmed him or her because of unfavorable attempts to develop relationships.[9] People who are isolated because of their attempts to avoid pain have cut themselves off from an emotional and spiritual support that becomes critical when a crisis arises. There is a need for strong relationships starting with the individual's own family. The family system that has greater support has an easier time dealing with crisis or avoiding crisis situations altogether.[10]

As a step toward prevention, a counselor needs to encourage and assist individuals who tend to isolate themselves. These loners need to move into relationships with others. People who can work through stressful situations with a network that is already in place have a much reduced chance of a crisis developing.

The individual who is new to a community may attend or join a church in part to establish new relationships. When a person is "checking" on a church he or she may be seeing if there are relationship possibilities. People often do not stay at a church because they feel they just don't fit in. The reality often is that they didn't find good support groups or they didn't feel they could break into preexisting groups. New members may greatly need to feel included as they work through the stress of moving, which might include new debt, new job, or family strain.

A new members' and/or an inquirers' class at the church can help new members develop friends rapidly without having to gain acceptance from the established member who has a friendship network that may not be very open to newcomers. When a church has sensitive leadership in such classes, Sunday school, or Bible study groups, the individual needing a support system or network can be integrated into the church. The church and its subsystems (i.e., youth group, missionary groups, Sunday school classes, Bible study) can be friendship centers for people who are new to the community or who have a significant need. Specific programs can be designed within the church for helping people develop interpersonal skills and building relationships. For example, growth groups led by a trained professional or other skilled persons can be offered.

When individuals in counseling with us have limited social skills and are isolated, we often prescribe their joining a group. As they get involved, we serve as coach, encourager, and sometimes healer when they face hurdles in specific relationships.

In chapter 10 we discuss the development of lay counselors. These helpers can be a great assistance to the person who has few other supportive relationships. If an individual is suicidal or otherwise threatening the well-being of self or others, most counselors or mental health professionals are in particular need of a group of people helpers.[11] The trained, lay crisis counselor can help during the height of a crisis and assist in prevention by helping the individual develop social skills and build supportive relationships which may provide life-saving resources.

Building Relationship with God

Lawrence Crabb has developed a model of counseling that seeks to "promote Christian maturity, to help people enter into a richer experience of worship and a more effective life of service."[12] The primary resource of the Crabb model is a dynamic relationship between God and the counselee. Most Christians have seen how powerful a dynamic relationship with God can be when an individual seems to be under pressure from all sides. Yet many in our churches are either new Christians or have not yet reached a level of spiritual maturity that is centered in a dynamic or meaningful two-way relationship with the triune God.

Medical doctors have often attested to the sustaining and healing power that can come from a relationship with God. Herbert Gaskill, M.D., stated, ". . . for most individuals religion is a resource which can be called upon to mobilize important strengths for facing crisis."[13]

It should be noted, however, that some people use religion rather than live it. Emil Brunner pointed out that the aim of religion is not to satisfy our wishes or to develop our personalities. He points out that a dynamic relationship with God means realizing his will and living accordingly.[14] When people attempt to use religion for their self-serving benefit, its power is very limited in dealing with stress. In other words, religion of itself is not enough in the face of crisis; it takes a dynamic relationship with God to find fully effective resolution of human crises.

Albert Outler has said that "the love born of Christian faith can be trusted to control and direct the psychic energies as nothing else can" (see 2 Cor. 5:14).[15] The new creature we become in Christ allows a person to love in such a way that he or she has a new power with which to manage stressors. This love is born of a reconciliation to God through Christ (2 Cor. 5:20, 21).

We've often encountered pastors in serious difficulty, frequently due to stressors within their churches or families. Charles Kemp has indicated that these problems can come from neglect of a pastor's own spiritual life.[16] If this is a problem for a pastor, then it can just as easily be for a layperson. There needs to be a devotional life that leads to a dynamic relationship with God if a person is to overcome stressful situations that have the potential of causing a crisis.

We have found several ways of preventing crisis through strengthening a person's spiritual life. You can help your clients to: 1. develop a growing, meaningful relationship with Jesus Christ; 2. live a value system that is consistent with personal beliefs; 3. deal forthrightly with sin in their lives; 4. allow the Holy Spirit to use them in helping others spiritually; 5. build a devotional life that includes prayer, Bible reading, and meditation.

Managing Environmental Factors that Cause Stress

Stress can be eliminated by altering one's environment.[17] In many cases, a change in these conditions alters the stressors that lead to crisis.

Helen was a very caring person who grew up in a family that had a very high regard for the medical professions. She struggled through school to receive her degree in nursing. For three years she worked at a hospital not far from her parents' home. Initially the excitement of the new job, the related economic rewards, and the sense of independence caused her to feel "upbeat" about her work, self, and those around her. Over a period of months she began to feel stressed in the job. She was working from 11:00 P.M. until 7:00 A.M. five days a week, plus she was taking one or two extra shifts each week to pay for furniture for her new apartment. She was tired a great deal of the time. It seemed as if the doctors were beginning to "snap" at her. She had no time for a social life. Helen's work was suffering. Her last few reviews were not nearly as good as those during the first months at the hospital. She was feeling enough stress that she could not sleep, so she started taking medication. As she put it, "I'm either feeling drained, depressed, or anxious." She was headed for a crisis.

The most immediate way of reducing the stress was to eliminate the extra shifts. By this one step alone she was able to relax a little, not feel so pressured, and have time for some social life. Life no longer was work, eat, sleep, and then work. Next she reevaluated her budget, cut some expenditures, and suddenly she was able to live on her base salary without overtime.

Helen was able to avert a crisis in her life by changing environmental stressors. In many situations, environmental change is the fastest way to reduce stress that is leading to a crisis.

Obviously, some environmental changes are difficult to make or do not fit into Christian values. For example, should a husband be actively abusing his wife, a counselor may not feel he or she should advise divorce. Yet even in these situations some environmental relief can be suggested that does fit within a specified value system.

Although it is not ideal, a couple may choose to separate briefly for a cooling off period. Change may involve removing oneself from sources of pain, fever, fatigue, exhaustion, extreme temperatures, or intense and intermittent noise.[18] The emphasis here is the importance of reducing stressors.

When a client is giving early warning signs of a developing crisis or when the individual has a low tolerance to stressors resulting in frequent crisis reactions, a list of all current stressors should be made, including physical conditions. Any stressors that can be removed or modified should be. This action can serve as a form of demystification. Often an individual can manage stress better if he or she knows the source or sources of the stress. As one client said, "I thought I was going crazy until you pointed out that my diet might be affecting my ability to deal with my children."

Changing environmental conditions and factors can reduce stress. As a prevention strategy, encourage and train people to avoid, to the degree possible, stressors in their lives. They need to see their choices clearly so they don't feel like victims of their circumstances. Some stress is unavoidable and other stress is valuable. The issue is management of stress and avoidance or reduction of unhealthy or nonvaluable stress.

Preventing Your Own Burnout

The counselor or pastor who deals with or supervises others who deal with crisis counseling needs to be especially sensitive to the occupational hazards of burnout, a common ailment of those who are over-committed and over-identified with those they are helping. Although burnout has always been an issue for those in the helping professions, it has been extensively addressed in the professional literature for only the past decade.[19]

The following is a list of common symptoms of burnout: lack of energy, excessive fatigue, irritability, extensive anxiety, impotence, futility, detachment, boredom, and powerlessness.

Often a person will not recognize the development of his or her own symptoms. We all need to remain open to the feedback of those around us, such as a spouse, family, or staff.

Why is the crisis counselor especially at risk for burnout? Several reasons tend to apply particularly to pastors. They often add crisis counseling onto a schedule that is already heavily loaded with people interaction. A pastor's time demands are extensive.[20] Unless a pastor has arranged some limitation, he or she is virtually on call twenty-four hours per day, seven days per week.[21]

Second, crisis counseling is especially emotionally intensive, at times involving life-or-death situations. Helping others through crisis produces more of an emotional drain than virtually any other professional activity.[22]

In many small churches, the pastor is not a part of a ministry team. Not being able to consult in confidence with a fellow staff professional results in a sense of isolation and may contribute to burnout.

Certain approaches and belief systems also can contribute to the emotional draining of the crisis counselor. When one takes upon oneself the responsibility for another's problem, burnout can occur. This need to control is directly related to a counselor's stress.[23] As we've said, the model of one being called alongside to help while the counselee maintains ownership of the crisis is best for all concerned.

Another belief, that the counselor can help every counselee rapidly and successfully resolve the crisis, also contributes to burnout. Not all counselees will be successful in resolving their crises. Some will get markedly better; some will make limited progress; others will get worse. Having realistic expectations as to the amount of progress clients will make is critical. We do not want to underestimate the power of God to intervene in any given situation, yet our observation is that people do not always make the choices we wish they would. Just as not everyone will respond to the gospel, not everyone will respond to crisis intervention. Perhaps the parable of the man sowing seeds in different soils is a model of what happens in crisis counseling (Luke 8:4–15). The Bible is loaded with examples of those who did not follow the clear instructions of God (i.e., Adam, Saul, David). None of us should assume that all will follow our encouragement either.

Burnout does not usually occur suddenly, but over a period of time. Therefore, if you realize this is happening, you have time to prevent its occurrence. Some have suggested that burnout occurs in a series of stages.[24] Perhaps one moves from enthusiasm to stagnation to frustration to apathy and finally ends up feeling hopeless. As one progresses through these stages one moves from high concern and emotional involvement with others to emotional isolation. Unfortunately, the emotional isolation affects not only one's relationship with counselees but also with parishioners, family, and friends. Eventually one may feel no concern for and/or avoid contact with others.

As one moves through these phases it is more and more difficult to regain energy and enthusiasm. The best possible solution to burnout, then, involves prevention, but the second best solution involves early intervention back at the frustration stage.[25] If you wait until you are thoroughly burnt out, you may need a longer period of structural recovery or rest.

Burnout does not have to occur even for those dealing extensively with crisis intervention. God well demonstrated his knowledge of humanity when he established the Sabbath as a day of rest "and made it holy"—rest can be holy! For pastors, the Sabbath is not a day of rest, but they can use the principle and take time off for renewal and relaxation.

Pastors and counselors need to set aside time when they can be away from the constant flow of demands. They need to develop and maintain relationships that provide emotional as well as professional support.[26] They need to build into their schedules time to interact with other professionals where mutual support can be received and given.[27]

It is also important not to work alone but to have a personal support system that is made up of fellow counselors, close friends, and family. Social support is associated with low levels of burnout and mental health problems resulting from job stress.

Professional pacing is an important concept. Those in the helping professions need to know their schedule limitations as to how many counseling sessions they can schedule per week. They owe it to the counselees they see not to schedule themselves beyond their limitations.[28] Sometimes this means finding alternative systems for delivery of counseling services or referral. You may have a tendency to attempt to help everyone and feel a sense of guilt if you have to miss seeing someone. I think we do need to remember that not even Jesus healed everyone. He did set limitations on his time and would leave the multitudes to be alone (Matt. 8:18–23).

You need time when you can be alone, go fishing, play golf, or fly a kite. You need time for spiritual, emotional, and physical renewal—if you are to prevent burnout.

Summary list of factors leading to burnout:

- not enough time for relaxation and rest
- not enough emotional support from others
- taking on oneself the counselee's problems
- seeing too many emotionally demanding crises in short time span
- unrealistic expectations relative to helping those in crisis

CHAPTER TEN

LAY CHURCH LEADERSHIP AND CRISIS SUPPORT

MANY CHRISTIAN WORKERS FACE periods when everything seems to be "breaking loose." At these times, people helpers may be in crisis themselves. Certainly they are under great stress, unless lay support people are available to help. Pastors normally rely on board members or other lay leaders for help, but most of these laypersons are not identified as lay counselors and have little or no formal training in crisis intervention. Pastors who have identified, carefully screened, trained, and developed lay people to help when everything is "breaking loose" are much more effective in their ministry than pastors who "wing it" when crisis occurs within the church family.

In this chapter we will explore the need for paraprofessional crisis counselors within the local church. We will also discuss a biblical and social basis for such workers. We will conclude with thoughts on selection process, training methods, resources, and administrative procedures necessary for a successful crisis counseling ministry.

Need for Paraprofessional Crisis Counselors

Pastors are confronted with two demands that often conflict with each other: the needs of an individual member or family and the needs of the congregation at large. The pastor may be torn between sermon preparation and serving the needs of one individual who is in crisis. The pastor who invests a prolonged amount of time with one member or one family may sense resentment from other members of the congregation. Misunderstandings might be reduced if a pastor could just report all the details of each crisis and thus explain why such a narrowed investment of time is important, but of course that would involve breaking professional ethical standards.

Fred Miller just completed his first year of his first pastorate: Westernbridge Community Church. He and Alice were married seven years ago, while he was in seminary. The people of Westernbridge loved their pastor. He was a good preacher. He visited church members regularly and was always very affirming. All was well until last month when everything appeared to "break loose." Mrs. Edwards called Pastor Fred on Friday morning just a month ago to let him know that her fourteen-year-old daughter, Betty, had run away from home. When Betty returned home, the pastor spent a great deal of time with mother, daughter, and the school counselor. Last week Fred learned from Mrs. Edwards that Betty had accused her twenty-year-old brother of sexually abusing her for nearly five years. Fred was overwhelmed with this family crisis.

Two days after Mrs. Edwards's first call, Alex Foster called to tell Fred that Alex had just learned that he had cancer of the bladder. Needless to say, Alex, his wife, and grown children were in a state of crisis. While Alex only attended church once in a great while, he needed help. Fred spent a considerable amount of time with Alex and/or his family, including most of the day Alex had surgery.

Two weeks ago Alma Jones came by Fred's office before the Sunday morning service to tell him that they had no savings left. Her husband had lost his job as a result of a strike last year and now they needed help from somewhere. The Jones family included three elementary-school-age children and they were already behind in the rental payments for their small apartment.

Within days of Alma's first discussion, she came by the office to tell Fred that her husband had been abusing her physically. She said that she couldn't take it anymore. Fred and Alice took Alma and children into their own home and Fred attempted to work with the husband. Fred felt like a circus juggler who was not keeping up with the balls.

In just a month Fred had experienced crisis-producing situations that were a real drain on his personal resources. He knew the quality of his sermons had slipped during the past several weeks and the next quarter of Sunday school was not yet planned. For a month he had not visited anyone but these people in crisis. People were starting to ask questions. A few began to complain. As if this was not enough, Alice was getting tired of Alma and the children living in the parsonage. Alice did not appreciate his being away so much nor the frequent calls at all hours of the night and day.

If Fred's situation continued, his marriage, his ministry, and his own health could be at stake. Pastors have watched their ministries unravel in similar times of multiple crisis situations. When additional problems exist in the church, the efforts of the good-hearted pastor can result in tragedy for all.

Pastors are less likely to be as overstressed as Fred if they have trained lay persons who can provide support for people in crisis. The pastor who has helpers can be an "act-er" rather than a reactor. Most pastors have run up against the limits of their time and energy. For this reason they have, possibly informally, formed a network of lay helpers who have certain spiritual gifts or who have demonstrated their caring for others. It appears wise for a church to have from three to five trained paraprofessional counselors for every two hundred members.

Some church members have unique and valuable knowledge because of their professions or occupations. Other church members have supportive personality traits or can be of great help because they have had certain life experiences. Many people in crisis respond better to people with whom they can identify, such as those who are of the same sex and/or age, or from a similar background.

Pastor Wright received a phone call from a church family. A young woman, Carol, had come "pounding" on their door begging for help. She'd said some people were threatening to hurt her because she would not do what they wanted her to do to get more money for drugs. Carol's erratic behavior indicated she was under the influence of a drug. The family did not know what to do. They were afraid for the young woman's well-being, yet they did not want to get in the middle of a drug-related problem and become bystander victims. Wisely, Pastor Wright started to put together a network to help Carol. He started with a church member who was a police officer knowledgeable about drug abuse and laws and resources that might relate to Carol's situation.

Pastor Wright also called a young woman in the church who was a recovered drug addict. Linda had been in the drug scene for nearly five years before she had become a Christian. Because of her background, Linda became a strong influence in Carol's life both by her teaching and modeling. Pastor Wright could never have filled Linda's role as he had come from a much different background. His ability to provide lay counseling support well depicts the type of ministry possible when a lay training program has been instituted.

The pastor who attempts to handle all the crises brought to him or her may soon burn out.

Basis for Lay Crisis Counseling

Writers such as Paul Miller, from their studies of Scripture and the history of the church, have emphasized the importance of God's people helping one another.[1] The Bible gives account after account of lay people (nonclergy) helping other members of the body of believers. The early church was known as a helping and sharing community (Acts 2:45–46). Through sermons and Christian education all members of a church can be encouraged to increase their awareness of and sensitivity to those going through crises. But specific members may be identified and specifically trained to assist those in crisis.

Jay Adams has stated that believers can be enablers of healing in crisis situations.[2] As its members are obedient to God, the church has within it the gifts, knowledge, and power to be a healing, helping, supporting body.

The church has been historically a lay and volunteer institution. Without volunteers who develop skills and achieve competency in essential areas of ministry, the church could not exist as it does today. Few, if any, churches can afford to pay members of the choir, Sunday school teachers, ushers and so forth. How many churches of five hundred members could afford a staff of six to ten counselors to meet crisis needs of those who turn to the church for help? The fact is that if the church is to meet the crisis-related needs of the people it serves, it will need to have lay volunteers. Today, and probably for as long as the church remains before Christ's return, laypersons will need to be an essential part of the counseling ministry of the church.

Since God gives gifts, talents, and personality traits that enable people without professional training to be healing agents, and since the church has historically relied upon these gifted people to minister, the church can and must continue to rely on laypersons if it is to be a wise steward of God's resources.

Selection of Lay Crisis Counselors

Properly starting a lay crisis counseling program involves carefully selecting counselors. A coordinator needs to consider who the candidates are and what they are like. Traits such as mercy, inner peace, joy, wisdom, insight, love, acceptance, and genuineness cannot easily be trained into the person, but potential counselors need to be selected because they have these qualities.

Gary Collins has presented some essential criteria for selecting lay counselors such as availability and successful self-management.[3] Candidates should be available on short notice, as crises, by their nature, present urgent needs. For example, a traveling salesperson, a student attending school in another state, and a retired person who travels a great deal might have great ability but their lack of availability would hinder their ministry.

It is important to select lay counselors who have successfully managed crises in their own lives. The individual who has had several recent crises which have not resulted in personal growth or the person who is currently in or recovering from a crisis situation is not a good candidate to be a crisis counselor. Often these people themselves need counseling and seminars or classes on personal crisis management. Simply stated, the person selected needs to be stable.

Most congregations require that key lay leaders, such as Sunday school teachers, be church members. This criterion for lay counselors makes a great deal of sense in that church members usually are required to state their belief in Jesus Christ and their agreement with the doctrinal statement of the local church. Church membership also is associated with accountability to the local body. Of course some churches have no formal system of membership and they might well measure a candidate by his or her active involvement in the body.

The lay counselor selected for training and service in crisis ministry needs to respect confidentiality. This may be a difficult character trait to measure unless the prospective counselor has been observed in a number of interpersonal situations in which he or she has not been the town gossip. Respect for another person's privacy is very important for the healing process and in avoiding the opening up of wounds. James 3:1–12 speaks of the significance of the tongue, which a prospective counselor must be able to bridle.

In *Christian Counseling,* Gary Collins suggests four motives that can create serious problems in counselors: 1. curiosity—the need for information; 2. the need for relationships; 3. the need for power; 4. the need to rescue.[4] These wrong motives can cause much difficulty. Therefore, it would be useful to screen out counselor candidates who are interested in counseling for these reasons.

Christ repeatedly spoke out against wrong motives (see Matt. 6:1–4). What type of motives should you look for in potential counselors? Often the very best counseling and most effective crisis intervention is done without fanfare or any visible recognition. The person who needs visible recognition and an abundance of "strokes" is generally not a good candidate. A crisis counselor needs to have a servant's heart as modeled by Christ (John 13:14, 15); service and love are the essential motives for effective crisis counselors.

An individual may have all the characteristics of a good crisis counselor and still be ineffective if he or she does not have gifts associated with the ministry of counseling. Certainly one needs to have the gifts of listening, compassion, empathy, assertiveness, organization, and internal strength. Necessary spiritual gifts would include teaching, healing, helps, and administration. Another measure of a lay crisis counselor candidate is the "fruit of the spirit" as described by Paul in his letter to the Galatians (Gal. 5:22, 23).

In summary, significant criteria for selecting crisis counselors are:

1. availability on short notice
2. demonstrated ability to manage own crisis
3. stability
4. active church involvement or membership
5. ability to maintain confidentiality
6. appropriate motivation
7. counseling gifts
8. evidence of fruit of Spirit

Training Lay Crisis Counselors

In the first book in this *Resources for Christian Counseling* series, Dr. Collins speaks of dividing training into three phases: "pretraining, training, and post-training."[5]

Pretraining

Specific pretraining can include a Sunday or week-night elective on stress management, crisis management and prevention, or related subjects. Another option is to cover the material in a nine-to-ten-hour Friday night and Saturday seminar or workshop. Other pretraining can take place through Sunday school classes, caring groups, and even in a sermon series.

Pretraining programs should deal with prevention, stress management, crisis management, and resource development (including spiritual resource development).

Pretraining programs can help you spot persons whose negative self-concept would make them unable to serve well as lay counselors and it can help strengthen people who already have healthy self-concepts so they would be more effective counselors.

"The effectiveness of helpers depends on how they choose to use themselves as instruments."[6] This statement suggests that prospective counselors need to know how they can be used and understand who they are as instruments. A violin can be used in many ways, but within limits. A French horn can be used many other and even similar ways, but its limits do determine the boundaries of its usefulness.

Training

The training phase requires planning and a development of resource materials. Ivey and Galvin have described a training format that is adaptable to programs for lay crisis counselors.[7] Their format consists of the teaching of a specific skill; the "students'" observation of an "expert" therapist modeling the skill. This is followed by a presentation or reading material, and then the students' immediate practice of the skill in small groups. This model is compatible with Lukens's proposal for training paraprofessional Christian counselors.[8] Dr. Lukens's fourth level, "Body Life Skills II," discusses the development of specific counseling skills necessary for lay crisis counselors. These specific skills are best taught one at a time in a series, as set forth by Galvin.

A word of caution should be included in all programs. No matter what training has been completed, lay counselors should consult with or make referrals to professionals when counselees appear to be in serious difficulty or when needs are beyond the scope of received training. Generally, the more people know about counseling, the more they are careful in what help they render—the more rapid they are to refer counselees to professionals.

Post-training

After the training phase comes the post-training phase which includes practice and supervision. Practice does produce growth in the caring counselor.

The lay crisis counselor should work with an experienced crisis counselor or a trained professional for some period of time. This is important not only to determine if the trainee is able to transfer learned skills to active situations, it also allows for evaluation of the trainee. If we are not mistaken, even the best selection process will not guarantee that the prospective lay crisis counselor has what it takes to be a helping person.[9] Competency, sensitivity, and personal strength need to be measured in the real world, even after formal training.

Training and growth should never end. In many professions, continuing education or recertification is required for the practitioner to continue rendering service. In a similar fashion, training and supervision should continue to be built into a paraprofessional or lay crisis counseling program. Periodic classes, consultation, supervision, and distribution of current literature in the field are important if a group of counselors is to meet needs effectively.

Models of a Lay Crisis Counseling Program

A crisis counseling ministry in the church can take many forms, but several models seem to be most functional for the local church.

The first model is a "self-contained" crisis intervention ministry, sponsored by a single church. Churches with several hundred active members seem to be the best candidates for a self-contained program (such churches often have more than one professional staff member, possibly a minister whose primary function is pastoral care and counseling). A staff member formally trained in counseling should be able to develop a sound program if he or she can set aside ten to twenty hours per week for several months. Counselors developing a church's crisis intervention ministry may find the following sequence of steps helpful.

1. Survey the need in the church and the community for a crisis intervention ministry.

2. As part of a church program, give one or two presentations on crisis-related community needs (this could be in a worship service, women's group, Sunday school class, and so forth).

3. If the above "tests" demonstrate need and interest in a ministry, then develop a formal proposal for the ministry to be presented to the church board or body that would authorize the ministry.

4. When the final draft of the program is approved, make plans to arrange for staffing. You or the person responsible for the program should attempt to locate resource people in the church and community who can develop and staff the pretraining, training, and post-training phases.

5. After the initial training staff has been engaged, continue to plan the entire first year of the program, outlining sessions in detail.

6. Conduct the pretraining sessions as previously covered in this chapter. The recruiting and screening process for lay counselors should be ongoing throughout these seminars.

7. Conduct training sessions once a week for ten to fifteen weeks. At about this time, promotion of the ministry needs to begin.

8. Conduct the post-training sessions as the new ministry is being aggressively promoted to church members. With effective promotion, there should be enough demand for service that counselors will gain meaningful experience under professional staff supervision.

9. Continuing administration of the ministry requires good promotion, ongoing training, and excellent supervision.

A second model is for a crisis intervention ministry formed by a group of churches that band together. One of the churches may be assigned overall operational administration, while the other churches support with volunteers, friends, and promotion, using steps similar to the ones in the first church model. A variation on the multi-church model is where the churches band together to form and equally support a self-contained ministry. A non-profit corporation may be formed with a board made up of representation from each church. Such a group might provide additional benevolent services to the community at large (a hot-line, professional counseling, and so forth). In some communities, the ministerial association has been associated with or has been the catalyst for several such programs.

The third model is for churches to support an existing organization in the community that either already offers crisis counseling services or is willing to develop such a program. In addition to volunteer help, such a group would need financial assistance from churches who would benefit from and/or sponsor the program.

No matter which model is used, it is important that the crisis program be reevaluated at specified intervals and that its structure include a system of accountability. It is very easy for a program to fall into ineffectiveness after a few years. As the newness and excitement associated with the formation of a crisis intervention ministry fades away, mediocrity can slip in and cause a great deal of damage.

Conclusion

All churches are faced with the question, "How are we going to help our people and our neighbors face their inevitable crises?"

Churches can develop an effective crisis counseling ministry. Within the body of believers there are people who have the gifts—the capacities to minister to people in crisis. Most churches have laypersons who are willing to help in this ministry if they can be properly trained.

The Good Samaritan is a picture presented by Christ as to how Christians—church members—should love and care for their brothers and sisters.

There is a need for crisis intervention in the church. There is a biblical basis for it, and people are able and willing to help and care. All that is needed for success is the decision to move ahead, develop the resources, and implement the plan for this vital ministry.

APPENDIX

VERSES FOR ENCOURAGEMENT

The following verses seem very helpful to share with those in crisis who are dealing with specific emotions. This topical list was prepared by Norman Wright and is quoted with permission.*

Comfort

Psalm 46:7	Psalm 103:17	Romans 8:38, 39
Numbers 14:9	Deuteronomy 31:6	Psalm 27:10
Psalm 73:23	Matthew 28:20	John 6:37–39
Isaiah 41:17	Psalm 94:14	

Peace

Romans 5:1, 2	Exodus 33:14	Psalm 85:8
Psalm 119:165	Isaiah 26:3	Isaiah 57:2
Isaiah 32:17	Matthew 11:29	Ephesians 2:14
Colossians 3:15	John 14:27	Numbers 6:24–26

Fear

Hebrews 13:6	Deuteronomy 7:21	1 Chronicles 16:25, 26
Jeremiah 15:20	Isaiah 41:10	Proverbs 16:7

*Wright, H. Norman, *Crisis Counseling*, 225–226, (San Bernardino, Calif.: Here's Life Publishers, 1985).

Isaiah 35:4
Nehemiah 4:14
Joel 3:16
2 Corinthians 1:10
Psalm 28:7
Psalm 4:8
Philippians 4:9
Deuteronomy 1:17
Psalm 56:3

Anxiety

Matthew 11:28
Job 34:12
Psalm 55:22
Proverbs 3:5, 6
John 16:33
Psalm 20:7
Psalm 86:7
Isaiah 40:11
Genesis 28:15
Psalm 50:15
Isaiah 41:13
Psalm 68:19

For those who feel weak

Psalm 142:3
Habakkuk 3:19
Psalm 72:13
Ephesians 3:16
Psalm 147:6
1 Chronicles 16:11
Psalm 55:18
2 Corinthians 12:9
Isaiah 57:15
Psalm 37:10, 11
Psalm 62:11
Jeremiah 10:6

Despair

Haggai 2:4
Isaiah 40:29
2 Thessalonians 3:3
Ephesians 1:18
Psalm 100:5
James 1:12
Isaiah 51:6
Hebrews 10:35
Psalm 46:1
Ezekiel 34:16
Daniel 2:23
Jeremiah 32:17
Psalm 119:116

Grief

Isaiah 43:2
Psalm 71:20, 21
Psalm 119:50
Psalm 116:15
Psalm 119:28
2 Corinthians 1:3, 4
Revelation 21:3, 4
Psalm 119:76
2 Thessalonians 2:16, 17

Times of trouble

Psalm 50:15
Psalm 9:12
Psalm 46:1
John 16:33
Psalm 37:39, 40
Psalm 138:7
Psalm 121:5–8
Psalm 34:7

Feeling desperate and depressed

Zephaniah 3:17
Psalm 30:5
Psalm 42:11
John 10:10
Psalm 34:18
Psalm 126:5
Psalm 40:1, 2

BIBLIOGRAPHY

The following books are recommended as resources for crisis counseling. They need to be read with discernment, since not all authors write from a salient Judeo-Christian value system.

Aguilera, Donna, and Messick, Janice. *Crisis Intervention*. St. Louis: C. V. Mosby Co., 1982.

Cohen, Lawrence; Claiborn, William; and Specter, Gerald. *Crisis Intervention: An Overview of Theory and Technique*. New York: Human Sciences Press, 1983.

Collins, Gary. *Christian Counseling: A Comprehensive Guide*. Waco, Texas: Word Books, 1980.

Crabb, Lawrence. *Effective Biblical Counseling*. Grand Rapids: Zondervan Publishing House, 1977.

Crow, Gary. *Crisis Intervention*. New York: Association Press, 1977.

Hoff, Lee Ann. *People in Crisis: Understanding and Helping*. Menlo Park, California: Addison-Wesley Publishing Co., 1978.

Jacobson, Gerald. *Crisis Intervention in the 80s*. San Francisco: Jossey-Bass, Inc., 1980.

Switzer, David. *The Minister as Crisis Counselor*. Nashville: Abingdon Press, 1974.

Wright, Norman. *Crisis Counseling*. San Bernardino, California: Here's Life Publishers, Inc., 1985.

NOTES

Introduction

1. Paul R. Amato, "An Investigation of Planned Helping Behavior," *Journal of Research in Personality* 19 (1985):232–252.
2. Linda L. Viney et al., "Crisis Intervention Counseling: An Evaluation of Long- and Short-term Effects," *Journal of Counseling Psychology* 32, no. 1 (1985):29–39.
3. Paul A. Hare and David Naveh, "Creative Problem Solving," *Small Group Behavior* 16, no. 2 (November 1985):123–138.

Chapter 1 The Dynamics of a Crisis

1. Paul A. Hare and David Naveh, "Creative Problem Solving," *Small Group Behavior* 16, no. 2 (November 1985):123–138.
2. T. Holmes and R. Rahe, "The Social Readjustment Rating Scale," *Journal of Psychosomatic Research* 11 (1967):212–218.
3. Lydia Rapoport, "The State of Crisis," *Social Science Review* 36, no. 2 (June 1962):211–217.
4. Donna Aguilera and Janice Messick, *Crisis Intervention* (St. Louis, Mo.: C. V. Mosby Co., 1982), 4.
5. Norman Wright, *Crisis Counseling* (San Bernardino, Calif.: Here's Life Publishers, 1985), 16, 17.
6. Margaret J. Lundberg, *The Incomplete Adult* (Westport, Conn.: Greenwood Press, 1974), 142, 143.

7. Albert Ellis, *Reason and Emotion in Psychotherapy* (Secaucus, N.J.: Lyle Stuart, 1962), 48.
8. G. Caplan, ed., *Child and Adolescent Psychiatry, Sociocultural and Community Psychiatry* (New York: Basic Books, 1974), 816.
9. Rapoport.
10. Aguilera and Messick, *Crisis Intervention*, 1.
11. Arthur M. Nezu, "Differences in Psychological Distress Between Effective and Ineffective Problem Solvers," *Journal of Counseling Psychology* 32, no. 1 (1985):135–138.
12. Wright, *Crisis Counseling*, 24.

Chapter 2 A Biblical View of Crisis

1. Leroy Eims, *The Lost Art of Disciple Making* (Grand Rapids: Zondervan Publishing House, 1978), 54.
2. Lester D. Crow, *Psychology of Human Adjustment* (New York: Alfred A. Knopf, Inc., 1956), 442.
3. Herbert C. Schulberg and Marie Killilea, eds., *The Modern Practice of Community Mental Health* (San Francisco: Jossey–Bass Publishing, 1982), 169.
4. Jim Petersen, *Evangelism as a Lifestyle* (Colorado Springs: Navpress, 1980), 112.

Chapter 3 Health-Related Crises

1. Gary Collins, *Christian Counseling: A Comprehensive Guide* (Waco, Tex.: Word Books, 1980), 397.
2. Lawrence H. Cohen, William L. Claiborn, and Gerald A. Specter, *Crisis Intervention* (New York: Human Sciences Press, 1983), 131.
3. John E. Lockman, "Factors Related to Patients' Satisfaction with Their Medical Care," *Journal of Community Health* 9 (1983): 91–109.
4. Collins, *Christian Counseling*, 399.
5. Lee Ann Hoff, *People in Crisis: Understanding and Helping* (Menlo Park, Calif.: Addison–Wesley Publishing Co., 1978), 160.
6. Cohen, Claiborn, and Specter, *Crisis Intervention*, 132.
7. Collins, *Christian Counseling*, 449.

8. Richard P. Barth and Steven P. Schenke, "Enhancing the Social Supports of Teenage Mothers," *Social Casework* 65, no. 9 (November 1984):523–531.

9. Michael J. Strube and Linda S. Barboue, "Factors Related to the Decision to Leave an Abusive Relationship," *Journal of Marriage and the Family* 46, no. 4 (November 1984):837–844.

10. B. E. Aguirre, "Why Do They Return? Abused Wives in Shelters," *Social Work* 30, no. 4 (July–August 1985):350–353.

11. Daniel G. Saunders, "Helping Husbands Who Batter," *Social Casework* 65, no. 1 (June 1984):347–353.

12. Hanila Zimrim, "Do Nothing but Do Something: The Effect of Human Contact with the Parent on Abusive Behavior," *The British Journal of Social Work* 4, no. 5 (October 1984):475–485.

13. Collins, *Christian Counseling,* 452.

14. Saunders, "Helping Husbands Who Batter."

15. Krystyna Nieradzek and Raymond Cochrane, "Public Attitudes towards Mental Illness: The Effects of Behavior Roles and Psychiatric Labels," *International Journal of Social Psychiatry* 31 (1985):23–32.

16. Hoff, *People in Crisis,* 163.

Chapter 4 People Crises

1. Elisabeth Kübler-Ross, *On Death and Dying* (New York: Macmillan, 1970).

2. R. McCorkle and Benoliel J. Quint, "Symptom Distress, Current Concerns, and Mood Disturbance after Diagnosis of Life-Threatening Disease," *Social Science and Medicine* 17, no. 7 (1983):431–438.

3. Lee Ann Hoff, *People in Crisis: Understanding and Helping* (Menlo Park, Calif.: Addison–Wesley Publishing Co., 1978), 222.

4. Lawrence H. Cohen, William L. Claiborn, and Gerald A. Specter, *Crisis Intervention* (New York: Human Sciences Press, 1983), 19.

5. C. M. Sanders, "Effects of Sudden Versus Chronic Illness Death on Bereavement Outcome," *Omega* 13, no. 3 (1982–1983): 227–241.

6. M. Roskin, "Buffers for the Bereaved: The Impact of Social Factors on the Emotional Health of Bereaving Parents," *International Journal of Social Psychiatry* 30 (Winter 1984):311–319.

7. Theresa A. Rando, "Bereaved Parents: Particular Difficulties, Unique Factors, and Treatment Issues," *Social Work* 30, no. 1 (January–February 1985):19–23.

8. Robert M. Counts and Anita Sacks, "The Need for Crisis Intervention During Marital Separation," *Social Work* 30, no. 2 (March–April 1985):146–150.

9. Gary Collins, *Christian Counseling: A Comprehensive Guide* (Waco, Tex.: Word Books, 1980), 192.

10. Donna Aguilera and Janice Messick, *Crisis Intervention* (St. Louis, Mo.: C. V. Mosby Co., 1982), 111.

11. George Rekers and Judson Swihart, *Making Up the Difference* (Grand Rapids: Baker Book House, 1984), 15.

12. Judson Swihart and Steven Brigham, *Helping Children of Divorce* (Downers Grove, Ill.: InterVarsity Press, 1982), 31.

13. Paul Ammons, Jose Nelson, and John Woodarski, "Surviving Corporate Moves: Sources of Stress and Adaptation among Corporate Executive Families," *Family Relations* 31 (1982):207–212.

14. A. S. Cook and D. J. Weigel, "Relocation and Crisis: Perceived Sources of Support, *Family Relations* 32, no. 2 (1983):267–273.

15. Stephen Singular, "Moving On," *Psychology Today* 17 (June 1983):40–43.

16. R. R. Sell and G. F. DeJong, "Deciding Whether to Move: Mobility, Wishful Thinking, and Adjustment," *Journal of Sociology and Social Research* 67, no. 1 (January 1983):146–165.

Chapter 5 Life-Cycle Crises

1. Francis E. Kobrin and Linda J. Waite, "Effects of Childhood Family Structure on the Transition to Marriage," *Journal of Marriage and the Family* 46, no. 4 (November 1984):807–816.

2. Margaret and Gordon Nelson, "Problems of Equity in the Reconstituted Family: A Social Exchange Analysis," *Family Relations* 31 (1982):223–231.

3. J. Wallerstein and J. Kelly, "Children and Divorce: A Review," *Social Work* 24, no. 6 (November 1979):468–475.

4. Andres Cherlin and James McCarthy, "Remarried Couple Households: Data from the June 1980 Current Population Survey," *Journal of Marriage and the Family* 47, no. 1 (February 1985):23–30.

5. Jay D. Teachman and Alex Heckert, "The Impact of Age and Children on Remarriage: Further Evidence," *Journal of Family Issues* 6, no. 2 (June 1985):185–203.

6. Jay Belsky, Maureen Perry–Jenkins, and Ann C. Crouter, "The Work–Family Interface and Marital Change Across the Transition to Parenthood," *Journal of Family Issues* 6, no. 2 (June 1985): 205–219.

7. Stephen Bell, John Bancroft, and Alistair Philip, "Motivation for Parenthood: A Factor Analytic Study of Attitudes toward Having Children," *Journal of Comparative Studies* 16, no. 1 (Spring 1985): 111–120.

8. Renee Hoffman Steffensmeier, "A Role Model of the Transition to Parenthood," *Journal of Marriage and the Family* 44, no. 2 (May 1982):319–334.

9. Patricia Noller and Stephen Bagi, "Parent–Adolescent Communication," *Journal of Adolescence* 8, no. 2 (1985):125–144.

10. Eugene Campbell, Gerald R. Adams, and William R. Dobson, "Familial Correlator of Identity Formation in Late Adolescence: A Study of the Predictive Utility of Connectedness and Individuality in Family Relations," *Journal of Youth and Adolescence* 13, no. 6 (December 1984):509–526.

11. Dolores C. Borland, "A Cohort Analysis Approach to the Empty Nest Syndrome Among Three Ethnic Groups of Women," *Journal of Marriage and the Family* 44, no. 2 (May 1982):319–334.

12. D. J. Cheal, "Intergenerational Family Transfers," *Journal of Marriage and the Family* 45, no. 4 (November 1983):805–813.

13. Christopher S. Davies, "The Throw Away Culture: Job Detachment and Rejection," *The Gerontologist* 25, no. 3 (June 1985): 228–231.

14. Eloise J. Calvedt and Geoffrey Leigh, "Parent–Adult–Child Interaction and Psychological Well-being of the Elderly," *Family Perspective* 18, no. 3 (Summer 1984):93–100.

15. Harriet Rzetelny, "Emotional Stresses in Later Life," *Journal of Gerontological Social Work* 8, no. 314 (Spring–Summer 1985): 141–152.

16. Carroll Kennedy, *Human Development: The Adult Years and Aging* (New York: Macmillan Publishing Co., 1978), 299.

17. Elizabeth S. Johnson and Donald L. Spence, "Adult Children and Their Aging Parents: An Intervention Program," *Family Relations* 31, no. 1 (January 1982):115–122.

18. Yael Kremer, "Predictions of Retirement Satisfaction: A Path Model," *International Journal of Aging and Human Development* 20, no. 2 (1984–1985):113–122.

19. Eileen Harnsey, "Health Education in Preretirement Education—A Question of Relevance," *Health Education Journal* 41, no. 4 (1982):107–113.

20. Edith M. Freeman, "Multiple Losses in the Elderly: An Ecological Approach," *Social Casework* 65, no. 5 (May 1984):287–296.

Chapter 6 Financial Crises

1. Emmett J. Vaughan, *Fundamentals of Risk and Insurance* (New York: John Wiley and Sons, 1986), 329–332.

2. Sylvia Porter, *Sylvia Porter's Money Book* (Garden City, N.Y.: Doubleday and Company, Inc., 1975), 942.

3. Thomas E. Bailar et al., *Personal Money Management* (Chicago: Science Research Associates, Inc., 1969), 12.

4. Elvin F. Donaldson and John K. Pfahl, *Personal Finance* (New York: The Ronald Press, 1966), 52.

5. John Dollard et al., *Frustration and Aggression* (New Haven: Yale University Press, 1939), 132, 133.

6. G. Pirooz Sholevar, ed., *The Handbook of Marriage and Marital Therapy* (New York: S. P. Medical and Scientific Books, 1981), 522, 523.

7. S. Michael et al., "Rapid Response Mutual Aid Groups: A New Response to Social Crises and Natural Disasters," *Social Work* 30, no. 3 (May–June 1985):245–252.

8. David K. Switzer, *The Minister as Crisis Counselor* (Nashville: Abingdon Press, 1974), 61.

9. Leopold Bellak and Peri Faithorn, *Crises and Special Problems in Psychoanalysis and Psychotherapy* (New York: Brunner–Mazel Publishers, 1981), 206.

Chapter 7 Spiritual Crises

1. Everett F. Harrison, ed., *Baker's Dictionary of Theology* (Grand Rapids: Baker Book House, 1975), 338–341.

2. Carl M. Sweazy, *Evangelism That Evangelizes* (Ventura, Calif.: Clark's Printing Company, 1968), 82.

3. Gerald Richardson, "Crises Associated with the Christian Conversion" (D. Min. diss., California Graduate School of Theology, 1983), 132.

4. T. Lang and J. Hadden, "Religious Conversion and the Concept of Socialization: Integrating the Brainwashing and Drift Models," *Journal for the Scientific Study of Religion* 2, no. 1 (March 1983):9.
5. Gary Collins, *Christian Counseling* (Waco, Tex.: Word Books, 1980), 84.
6. Bruce Narramore and Bill Counts, *Guilt and Freedom* (Santa Ana, Calif.: Vision House, 1974), 154.

Chapter 8 Counseling Techniques for Crisis Intervention

1. Linda L. Viney et al., "Crisis Intervention Counseling: An Evaluation of Long- and Short-term Effects," *Journal of Counseling Psychology* 32, no. 1 (1985):29–39.
2. Lawrence Cohen, William L. Claiborn, and Gerald A. Specter, *Crisis Intervention* (New York: Human Sciences Press, Inc., 1983), 16.
3. Lee Ann Hoff, *People in Crisis: Understanding and Helping* (Menlo Park, Calif.: Addison-Wesley Publishing Co., 1978), 52.
4. Lester D. Crow, *Psychology of Human Adjustment* (New York: Alfred A. Knopf, Inc., 1956), 21.
5. Donna Aguilera and Janice Messick, *Crisis Intervention* (St. Louis, Mo.: C. V. Mosby Co., 1982), 62.
6. Marilyn A. Rumelhart, "When Understanding the Situation Is a Real Problem," *Social Casework* 65, no. 1 (January 1985):27–33.
7. Joseph F. Madonia, "Clinical and Supervisory Aspects of Crisis Intervention," *Social Casework* 65, no. 6 (June 1984):364–368.
8. Gary Collins, *Christian Counseling: A Comprehensive Guide* (Waco, Tex.: Word Books, 1980), 50.
9. Benjamin Gottlieb, "Assessing and Strengthening the Impact of Social Support on Mental Health," *Social Work* 30, no. 4 (July–August 1985):293–300.
10. Claire Rabin et al., "Refocusing from Child to Marital Problems Using the Marriage Contract Game," *Journal of Marital and Family Therapy* 11, no. 1 (1985):75–85.
11. William J. Doherty et al., "Emphasis on the Major Family Therapy Models: A Family FIRO Model," *Journal of Marital and Family Therapy* 11, no. 3 (1985):299–303.
12. Robert Eliot, "Helpful and Nonhelpful Events in Brief Counseling Interviews: An Empirical Taxonomy," *Journal of Counseling Psychology* 32, no. 3 (1985):307–322.

13. Richard Tolman and Sheldon D. Rose, "Coping with Stress: A Multimodel Approach," *Social Work* 30, no. 2 (March–April 1985): 151–159.

14. Norman Wright, *Crisis Counseling* (San Bernardino, Calif.: Here's Life Publishers, Inc., 1985), 41.

15. Phyllis Ashinger, "Using Social Networks in Counseling," *Journal of Counseling and Development* 63 (April 1985):519–521.

16. Gottlieb, "Assessing and Strengthening the Impact."

17. M. Jones and N. Stewart, "Helping the Environment Help the Client: A Sequenced Change Process," *Personnel and Guidance Journal* 58 (1980):501–506.

18. Ashinger, "Using Social Networks."

Chapter 9 Prevention of Crises

1. Gary R. Collins, *Innovative Approaches to Counseling* (Waco, Tex.: Word Books, 1986), 91, 92. An excellent discussion of goals is contained in this, the first in this *Resources for Christian Counseling* series.

2. David G. Benner, ed., *Baker's Encyclopedia of Psychology* (Grand Rapids: Baker Book House, 1985), 1130.

3. Norman Farberow, ed., *The Many Faces of Suicide* (New York: McGraw-Hill, 1980). The reference is from "Indirect Self-Destructive Behavior" as reported by T. M. Johnson.

4. Ibid.

5. David K. Switzer, *The Minister as Crisis Counselor* (Nashville: Abingdon Press, 1974), 46, 47.

6. Arnold Goldberg, ed., *Progress in Self Psychology,* 2 vols. (New York: The Guilford Press, 1985), 1:80.

7. Benner, *Baker's Encyclopedia of Psychology,* 1036.

8. Michael Hersen et al., eds., *The Clinical Psychology Handbook* (New York: Pergamon Press, 1983), 720.

9. Robert White, *The Enterprise of Living* (New York: Holt, Rinehart and Winston, 1976), 327, 328.

10. Roseanne Umana et al., *Crisis in the Family* (New York: Gardner Press, Inc., 1980), 1.

11. Leopold Bellak and Peri Faithorn, *Crises and Special Problems in Psychoanalysis and Psychotherapy* (New York: Brunner–Mazel Publishers, 1981), 111.

12. Lawrence J. Crabb, *Effective Biblical Counseling* (Grand Rapids: Zondervan Publishing House, 1977), 29.

13. Dana L. Farnsworth and Francis J. Braceland, eds., *Psychiatry, the Clergy, and Pastoral Counseling* (Collegeville, Minn.: St. John's University Press, 1969), 52.

14. Richard McCann, *The Churches and Mental Health* (New York: Basic Books, Inc., 1962), 11.

15. Albert C. Outler, *Psychotherapy and the Christian Marriage* (New York: Harper & Row Publishers, 1954), 221.

16. Charles F. Kemp, *The Caring Pastor* (Nashville: Abingdon Press, 1985), 143.

17. Wright, *Crisis Counseling,* 204, 205. In this section he gives two additional ways of dealing with stress: working on the symptoms and altering beliefs, negative thinking, and assumptions that leave a person vulnerable to stress.

18. Leo Goldberger and Shlomo Breznitz, eds., *Handbook of Stress: Theoretical and Clinical Aspects* (New York: The Free Press, 1982), 107.

19. Donna Aguilera and Janice Messick, *Crisis Intervention* (St. Louis, Mo.: C. V. Mosby Co., 1982), 179.

20. Gary L. Harbaugh and Evang Rogers, "Pastoral Burn out: A View from the Seminary," *Journal of Pastoral Care* 38, no. 2 (June 1984):99–106.

21. Diane McDermott, "Professional Burn out and Its Relation to Job Characteristics, Satisfaction, and Control," *Journal of Human Stress* 10, no. 2 (Summer 1984):79–85.

22. Steve Weinberg, Gary Edwards, and William E. Garove, "Burn out among Employees of State Residential Facilities Serving Developmentally Disabled Persons," *Children and Youth Services Review* 5, no. 3 (1983):239–253.

23. Rita E. Numerof and Michael N. Abrams, "Sources of Stress among Nurses: An Empirical Investigation," *Journal of Human Stress* 10, no. 2 (Summer 1984):88–100.

24. Aguilera and Messick, *Crisis Intervention.*

25. Susan G. Forman, "Occupational Stress Management: Cognitive–Behavioral Approaches," *Children and Youth Services Review* 5, no. 3 (1983):277–287.

26. Terry E. Carillio and David M. Eisenberg, "Using Peer Support to Prevent Worker Burn out," *Social Casework* 65, no. 5 (May 1984):307–310.

27. Lorraine Taylor and Spencer J. Salend, "Reducing Stress-

related Burn out through a Network Support System," *Pointer* 24, no. 4 (Summer 1983):5–9.

28. Robert L. Veninga, "Burn out and Personality," *Clinical Gerontologist* 2, no. 2 (Winter 1983):61–63.

Chapter 10 Lay Church Leadership and Crisis Support

1. Paul M. Miller, *Peer Counseling in the Church* (Scottdale, Pa.: Herald Press, 1978), 14.

2. Jay E. Adams, *Lectures on Counseling* (Grand Rapids: Baker Book House, 1978), 79.

3. Gary Collins, *Innovative Approaches to Counseling* (Waco, Tex.: Word Books, 1986), 34, 35.

4. Gary Collins, *Christian Counseling* (Waco, Tex.: Word Books, 1980), 34, 35.

5. Collins, *Innovative Approaches to Counseling,* 79.

6. Arthur W. Combs and Donald L. Avila, *Helping Relationships: Basic Concepts for the Helping Professions* (Boston: Allyn and Bacon, Inc., 1985), 191.

7. Dale Larson, ed., *Teaching Psychological Skills* (Monterey, Calif.: Brooks–Cole Publishing Co., 1984), 209. See also Eldon K. Marshall, et al., eds., *Interpersonal Helping Skills* (San Francisco: Jossey-Bass, 1982), 471–481.

8. Horace C. Lukens, Jr., "Training of Paraprofessional Christian Counselors: A Proposed Model," *Journal of Psychology and Christianity* 2 (1983):61–66.

9. Jane Allyn Piliavin et al., *Emergency Intervention* (New York: Academic Press, 1981), 185.

INDEX

Judson J. Swihart

Judson J. Swihart has a Ph.D. in human development and family studies from Kansas State University. He is also a licensed clinical social worker with many years experience in both family and individual counseling. In addition to both professional journal articles and popular articles, he has written several books, including *How Do You Say I Love You?*

Dr. Swihart is an assistant professor (part time) in the department of human development and family studies at Kansas State University and is the director of International Family Center in Manhattan, Kansas.

He and his wife, Nancy, live on a farm near Manhattan, Kansas, along with their two sons, Derrick and Dan, and their daughter, Sara.

Gerald C. Richardson

Gerald C. Richardson, D. Min., is president of the Growing Edge Counseling Center in Arcadia, California, and is a licensed marriage, family, and child counselor. For six years he served as pastor of Foothill Baptist Church in Sylmar. Dr. Richardson earned the master's degree in marriage, family, and child counseling from Azusa Pacific University and his doctorate in ministry from the California School of Theology. He was a contributor to the *Christian Life Study Bible* and has written a number of magazine articles on crisis counseling. He and his wife Jo Ann have four children and live in Northridge, California.